STUMBLING ON GOD

Christopher Burdon

STUMBLING ON GOD

Faith and vision in
Mark's Gospel

William B. Eerdmans Publishing Company
Grand Rapids, Michigan

First published in Great Britain 1990 by
SPCK
Holy Trinity Church
Marylebone Road
London   NW1 4DU

This edition published 1990
by special arrangement with SPCK by
William B. Eerdmans Publishing Co.
255 Jefferson Ave. SE
Grand Rapids, Michigan 49503

Printed in the United States of America

ISBN 0-80280493-4

Contents

Acknowledgements

Thanks are due to the following for permission to reproduce copyright material:

Faber and Faber, and Harcourt Brace Jovanovich, Inc, Orlando, Florida for the extract from T. S. Eliot's 'East Coker' in *Collected Poems 1902–62*.

Faber and Faber, and Oxford University Press, New York for the extract from Edwin Muir's 'The Killing' in *Collected Poems*.

Gwydion Thomas for the extracts from R. S. Thomas's 'H'm' and 'Pilgrimages' in *H'm* and *Frequencies*, published by Macmillan.

ICS Publications, 2131 Lincoln Road, N.E. Washington, D.C. 20002 for the extract from *The Collected Works of St John of the Cross*, trs. Kieran Kavanaugh and Otilio Rodriguez © 1979 by Washington Province of Discalced Carmelites.

Preface

Stumbling on God belongs to that parasitical species, books about books; though I hope it is about other things too, in particular about God and how we encounter him. But because the material I am mainly working with is St Mark's Gospel, it is important that before reading *this* book you first read or reread Mark's—ideally by hearing it read aloud to a group.

I have written in a way that is both 'pastoral' and 'critical'. No doubt this will seem too pastoral to some and too critical to others; but I am obstinate in believing that readers of the Bible need to let their whole imagination and intelligence loose on its words, and that any approach which tries to be purely devotional or purely literary or purely historical will be at least partly defective.

Most biblical quotations are from the Revised Standard Version, though for Mark I have often used my own even more literal translation. I have not wanted to burden the book with footnotes or references, but those who are familiar with writing about the New Testament will recognize my debt to many who have pondered the Gospels much more deeply than I, especially to R. H. Lightfoot, Austin Farrer, Dennis Nineham and Frank Kermode. A list of some books I have found useful is given at the back.

Two assumptions I have made, both of them in line with the findings of most if not all modern New Testament scholars. The first is that Mark's was the earliest Gospel to be written and that it was used by Matthew, Luke and possibly John; the second that Mark deliberately ended his book with the words 'for they were afraid' (16.8), so that in its original form it contains no appearances of the risen Jesus.

I owe much to all who over the years have taught me to read

Stumbling on God

and write and think and pray, first to my parents, then in particular to Michael Craze, William Wheeldon and Sr Jane SLG. Some of the thoughts here began in a clergy seminar and were published in an article in *Theology* in March 1987. I am grateful to the editors of that journal and especially grateful as well to John Fenton, who has given me so much encouragement and gracious advice over the past four years, and to Judith Longman of SPCK, who first persuaded me that there could be a book there and has since been so supportive to a nervous author. Pam Ward, John Hadley and James Ramsay also looked at earlier drafts of this book, and I am indebted to them for their comments. My warm thanks go to Moira Lovell, who typed the book, and to the Culham Educational Foundation, whose financial support enabled me to take some time away from pastoral duties; nor would this have been possible without the indulgence of my parishioners, colleagues and bishop.

Above all, I thank Rosemary, Sara, Eleanor and Jessica for putting up with me when I have been a rather useless companion absorbed in ancient words. I hope that they and you will feel that the absorption is of some value.

Christopher Burdon
July 1989

Introduction *The Taming of Terror*

While I was in Wales rereading St Mark's Gospel and thinking about this book I walked to the beach on a day when there was a powerful westerly gale. In a mood of crazed exhilaration I ran into the sea, forgetting to remove the glasses on which I depend for any vision that is not hopelessly myopic. Within half a minute of course they had been swept off my nose by a six-foot wave, and I was left groping and staggering in the water. My daughters and I scoured the shore at high tide and at low tide, but the glasses were no doubt smashed deep in the Irish Sea.

That moment produced the disjunction between sight and blindness that I had just been reading of 'by the sea' in Galilee. 'Do you still not understand?' the thundering waves were asking me, as Jesus had asked his fumbling half-blind disciples. Those men had heard and witnessed things that the Gospel-writers saw as words of life and events of salvation; but, at any rate according to Mark, they made little of them. Most of the time Jesus appears to have been speaking into the wind. Why did people who admired him and kept close to him miss his meaning and resist his way? Why, on the other hand, did the occasional outsider respond to him immediately with faith and understanding? And why today is a story or belief radiantly true to one person and infuriatingly obscure to her neighbour?

There are parables all about us, they are strewn on our shores. But so often we see without seeing and hear without hearing. It is as though the sea which could speak to us just makes a dull moaning, as though the sand which could shine is just a formless floor. Those who, like me, depend on glasses will know that when

1

you remove them the light of a street-lamp or a candle appears larger, more sparkling. Can it be that to perceive the reality hidden in the objects and happenings about us, to grasp parables, we need to have the spectacles of our conventional vision dashed from us?

Reading aloud 'the gospel'—that is, the little chunk of Matthew, Mark, Luke or John appointed for a particular day—is one of the traditional functions of a deacon or priest; and ever since I was made a deacon fifteen years ago I have performed this duty with some trepidation, sensing that the familiar words I am pronouncing hold a glory and a terror that challenge our customary ways of hearing and living. After returning from Wales to England, equipped with a new pair of glasses, I arranged to read aloud to a group not just a chunk but the whole of St Mark's Gospel. For me and for most who listened this was a new and powerful experience. True, 'the gospel' is hardly new. It is the 'old, old story' whose episodes and characters were well known to all those listeners. Even hearing it read aloud is nothing new, for Christian worshippers hear 'the holy gospel' read each Sunday and their preachers interpret it again and again. I sometimes suspect that if Mark or Luke were to creep into a modern church and hear the pastor reading and preaching about the parable of the sower or the prodigal son they might say, 'Hey, I wrote that one down: haven't they found any fresh parables in 1,900 years?' Yet, as our group found, there is freshness, there is power in the whole story: something that is good news, to be proclaimed not just received, though something that is maddeningly hard to define. And I sense that this must be to do not only with the way the Gospels are written but also with the man they are written about.

A sceptic (such as I often am) might respond that all this sense of power and mystery is just a hangover from the reverence with which the old, old story has been treated during the Christian centuries; that that story is impossible to verify historically and derives from primitive people who believed in angels, demons and nature miracles; that our reaction to it is no different in kind from our reaction to other stories or dramas which project us into a temporary world of exaggeration and magic. We may be

2

entertained, exhilarated, even enlightened by the experience, but the real world is the one *outside* the story. Yet this hardly does justice to the haunting way this particular story impels us into our world to change it, nor to the conviction of even a sceptical Christian that this man Jesus matters in a way that Odysseus and Hamlet do not matter. And if he still matters today, can we escape those strange first-century books called 'Gospels'?

St Mark, whoever he was, may have been the first person to apply the word 'gospel' (*euangelion*, good news) to the story of Jesus' travelling, teaching and healing. Until he wrote, *euangelion* had probably been used only of the preaching that through Jesus' death and resurrection God had given new hope and new life. But Mark heads his whole book 'the good news of Jesus the Messiah, the Son of God'. He is directing his readers to find new hope and new life not just in the resurrection of Jesus or in belief about that resurrection but in the whole story that leads up to it—in the preaching and death of John the Baptist, in Jesus' healing and exorcizing, in his teaching and arguing and journeying and dying. Matthew, Luke and John alter and expand Mark in all sorts of ways, but for them too the whole story matters. They are evangelists, they write their books and want them to be read so that the hearers can encounter God.

It has been fashionable among theologians in the 1980s to see the encounter with God mediated supremely through 'story'. This is a refreshing approach after wading through piles of philosophical arguments or dogmatic manuals, though it is sometimes exaggerated—after all, image, symbol and even proposition can reveal as well as story, and while much of the Bible consists of narrative by no means all of it does. But to seek truth in story begs other questions. What story? If it is partly or wholly the old one of Jesus, how is that to be heard and translated? This is a question not just for linguists and preachers but for anybody who thinks Jesus matters. For if what we hear of him is to be gospel as well as story, it must judge and challenge and encourage us. What the modern world usually seeks from its stories, however, is entertainment rather than good news. The theologian's picture of imaginative story-telling around a cosmic camp-fire is an attractive one; but the reality of story today is more likely to be that of the nuclear family or the solitary shift-worker crouched daily in front of the television soap opera before facing again the wrangles over money and sex or the noisy tedium of the factory. The story protects us from the banality outside. As 'entertainment' the Gospels can hardly compete, however hard the Church tries to domesticate their God and make his story enticing, for they were written with a purpose opposite to that of the soap opera, not to divert but to convert.

That is not to say that diversion is worthless or sinful. But it does suggest that the need for 'entertainment' as a particular function of life is a sign of human disintegration. In order to bear very much reality most of us need a fantasy-world: one that is easy to enter since, unlike more primitive myth, it incorporates outward features of our 'real' contemporary surroundings, but one that rarely threatens our identity or opinions or way of life since, again unlike myth, it excludes the heights of wonder and the depths of dread which can engage our whole psyche. We should not blame the media for this flight from reality. They are merely effective vehicles (more effective or at any rate more popular than religion, it appears) for temporarily removing the pain and injustice and purposelessness that lurk below the surface of our life. In any case, television and theatre do not only entertain; they can inform and challenge and even exalt us. But here too—after a harrowing performance of *King Lear* or an uncompromising documentary on world economics—many of us quickly revert to small talk. Is this because we are aware that we have encountered a truth too massive for us to grasp, a truth that sits ill at ease with the less momentous but real concerns of our lives?

Yet the massive truth and the everyday concerns need not exclude each other. In all the first three Gospels the scene of greatest exaltation in the whole story, known as Jesus' transfiguration, is deliberately juxtaposed with a scene of violent human terror, the raving of an epileptic boy and his father's desperate cry for help. Peter and James and John have been with Jesus on the mountain. There they cowered 'exceedingly afraid' as he appeared in unearthly whiteness and as together they were enveloped in the cloud that is the glory of the invisible God. But as they descend from this terrible exaltation in the heavenly world another terror rages at the foot of the mountain. The possessed boy thrashes about in convulsions, his father screams and the other disciples argue with the scribes; all grow helpless and enraged, yet into this chaotic human mêlée is thrust the exalted Jesus, declared God's Son. The Gospel-writers—above all Mark, who tells the two-part story with the greatest detail and excitement—believe that the same Jesus is at home in both the heavenly and the earthly terror. And the implication is that so should his followers be: rooted in heaven and in earth, not floating in an atmospheric layer of their own construction.

Yet despite the repeated reading of the Gospels and the honour given to Jesus, the Church often adapts his story and his image to function as entertainment. It can itself provide us with a fantasy-world to protect us from both the glory and the terror where the Lord of the Gospels stalks. Perhaps this charge needs some elucidation. While most churchgoers are familiar with complaints that services are boring and that the people who frequent them are gloomy, I was struck recently by a remark from someone who told me that she had left the Church because it was all too *happy*. It emerged that she was not just objecting to the charismatic fashions of arm-waving and hand-clapping but as a matter of deeply-felt principle to what she saw as the Church's determination to conceal all traces of evil and conflict. Terrified that its story and dogmas might not fit the world's experience of reality, the Church conspired, she claimed, to alter that reality. So from Sunday school songs to funeral sermons to episcopal moral directives an impression was given that all was really good in the creation of the good God and that a benign Saviour would remove any trace of ill. True, sin and suffering entered the story, but only as counters to be pushed aside by the masterstroke of resurrection. And while she was still attracted by the figure of Jesus, she was not prepared to go along with such a mangling of reality in his name; the music of Beethoven or a good game of tennis were more exalting for her than bland promises of forgiveness and paradise, and engagement with the real suffering and injustice of the known world more redemptive than a crucifixion reversed by a piece of magic.

The charge may have been crudely put and the pathology of

modern Christianity offered by my friend may seem an extreme one, though perhaps the Church's usual defence mechanisms are hardly less crude. Certainly I know as a pastor how, wishing to keep their members and to attract new ones, the churches slip easily into a world of inoffensive diversions. Better by far, goes the unspoken thought, to provide innocent religious comfort than to risk institutional irrelevance and financial instability by handling those awkward themes of glory, sacrifice, evil, death and judgement that haunt the Bible. Religion as entertainment—a decorous and pleasantly archaic adjunct to everyday life, rather like madrigals or thatched cottages—carefully evades the extremes of glory and terror, censoring from the Bible those translucent images of heaven and those bloody images of earth to preserve an undemanding half-world of friendly Father, gentle Jesus and caged Spirit, where love itself is reduced from a passionate divine fire to polite good-neighbourliness, and righteousness from the just ordering of the intractable world to personal rectitude.

The Swiss theologian Karl Barth was once asked by a newspaper to reply to an article by a professor of philosophy which urged the necessity of atheism; his response concluded with the avowal that he was far less worried by the professor's theoretical atheism than by the 'real enemy' of practical atheism,

> the 'Christianity' that professes faith in God very much as a matter of course, perhaps with great emphasis, and perhaps with righteous indignation at atheism wild or mild, while in its practical thinking and behaviour it carries on exactly as if there were no God. It professes its belief in him, lauds and praises him, while in practice he is the last of the things it thinks about, takes seriously, fears or loves. God is thus turned into an item in the inventory of the contents of an old-fashioned or partially modernized house, a piece of furniture the owner would refuse to part with in any circumstances, but for which he has nevertheless ceased to have any real use; or rather, which he has very good reasons for taking care not to use, for it might be uncomfortable or dangerous. God is spoken of, but what is meant is an idol that one treats as one sees fit.

Jesus too has often been turned by Christians into a sort of redundant idol or picturesque demigod—a very convenient object of esteem, since it binds us close neither to the mystery of God nor to the reality underfoot. Such a Christ still flourishes in the sexless creature seen blessing children or standing by tombs in innumerable Victorian church windows, who proves by his static pose and weird clothing that he is not really human and by his undisturbing gaze that he is not really divine. Here is a being who could never have called Herod 'that fox' or thrown the traders out of the Temple, let alone got himself crucified.

Now the curious thing about this 'Christ', neither God nor man, is that many of his worshippers are fervent in their adherence to the orthodox doctrine of incarnation, according to which divine and human nature are inseparably united in the one Lord Jesus Christ. The form of the doctrine is retained but its reality is tamed. For it speaks of the enfleshment of the Word of God, that is, of divine activity's invasion of our physical, secular world; of God's placing himself on our level and in our reach, so to speak, yet without abandoning his mystery—'one and the same Christ ... made known in two natures without confusion, without change ...', stated the Council of Chalcedon—so that we can encounter but not possess him. Filled with the human lust for possession, we find this elusive God-man hard to respond to. So traditionally Christians have identified more easily with the Mary of the crib, embracing the baby, or with the Mary of the *Pietà*, embracing the corpse, than with Mary at the cross, separated from her dying yet still living Son. The former two are scenes easy to fix in time and easy to sentimentalize, scenes where the Christ can be held motionless and asleep in infancy or in death so that he does not fix us with his gaze or call us to discipleship. We may make edifying meditations on his humility, but we are not challenged by the 'imperious ruler' of whom Albert Schweitzer wrote and by whom he was drawn and driven.

As well as being a form of self-protection, does this timidity of response stem from an unwillingness to read the Bible attentively? Most of the New Testament is a poetry born of the terror, joy and controversy springing from encounter with God through Jesus; yet both scholars and 'the faithful' (who may despite suspicions on both sides be the same people) tend to treat it primarily as a textbook of historical facts and theological propositions. Of course the Bible contains both of these, but above all it is to be read with the attention of heart and ear that we bring to poetry, abandoning the lust for certitude and letting the text question us rather than requiring it to answer our questions or even deciding in advance what answers it must give. It is the experience of being confronted by the stories of the Bible and by the Christ to whom in different ways they point that allows me to call the Bible 'the word of God'—that, rather than any theory of inspiration or doctrine of inerrancy. Again, since the Bible deals largely in archetypal images and in human stories it cannot be condensed into essential meaning or theological system; the meaning lies in the readers' encounter with the successive stories and images, not in some abstraction from them or cunning combination of them. In a way, the more educated reader of the Bible has the greater difficulty, especially if his education has been mainly scientific, for he expects to be able to explain things or expects the Bible to explain things for him. And the Bible refuses to co-operate with such a reader, since it does not treat God as an object of investigation but as subject of all reality and history; the object is the reader himself.

So the modern reader of the Bible is often in the position of the Pharisees as they are presented in the Gospels; asking a question and receiving for answer a riddle or another question. Jesus 'taught with authority', we are told; and with our emaciated modern conception of a teacher's vocation we therefore expect him to provide information, answer questions, propel us safely through the test of life. But we are disappointed in him, for his is a teaching of stories, riddles and parables, not of the straightforward doctrinal and ethical teaching that the Church today is frequently asked for and that at least parts of it readily supply. The answer of the catechism may satisfy the tidy mind. The question of the parable refuses to do so; instead of giving an explanation it asks us to think in a different way, challenging us (in the case of Jesus' parables) with news of 'the Kingdom', that is, of the simultaneous nearness and strangeness of God. Accustomed to instant colour pictures, our age needs to relearn the patience and imagination simply to listen to stories—not only the parables of Jesus, but the whole parable of Jesus himself, or

8

rather the four parables of Matthew, Mark, Luke and John, that cannot be compressed into a single synopsis or doctrinal scheme.

Even in the New Testament there are signs that the offence of Jesus is being softened. Already the tendency begins to turn the 'imperious ruler' into a moral exemplar or a doctrinal token. ('The Word made flesh here is made word again', as Edwin Muir was later to accuse Calvinism.) In Matthew he is presented as the new lawgiver, in Luke as the model of a righteous martyr, in John as a mystical presence. But none of these early tendencies can eradicate the impression, clearest of all in Mark, of a 'stumbling-block' disturbing his world with the nearness and justice of God. We try to edge round the stumbling-block or move it to the side of the road; even, as Schweitzer accused liberal theology of doing, to pulverize it into building materials to suit the architectural styles of our own age. But the stumbling-block cannot be so easily managed, nor can the many-sided Book which it straddles. Northrop Frye quotes 'a sardonic Old English riddle ... that begins "An enemy deprived me of life, took away my strength, then soaked me in water, then took me out again and put me in the sun, where I soon lost all my hair"'; and he comments,

> The answer is 'book', specifically a Bible codex. The riddle obliquely describes the method of preparing a codex in the writer's day, and seems to be referring also to the shearing of Samson in Judges 16.17–22. The normal human reaction to a great cultural achievement like the Bible is to do with it what the Philistines did to Samson: reduce it to impotence, then lock it in a mill to grind out our aggressions and prejudices. But perhaps its hair, like Samson's, could grow again even there.

My analysis so far of our treatment of the Christ and the Bible may seem unduly negative. But so concerned are we that the hair might grow and entangle us in its strength that we frequently shun our own imagination with the *pōrōsis* (hardness or blindness) for which Jesus upbraided his disciples. It is ironic that it is often those with the 'highest' doctrines of Christ or the Bible who are the keenest to trap them in the mill of their systems. The Bible is full of great concrete images, sparkling with the ambiguity that enlivens all great literature. The Church has loved to spiritualize those images, so that they can be tamed and manipulated to say what the insiders want them to say; but this can never be entirely successful, for the symbols and stories have a way of springing back to become a glass through which even outsiders can glimpse the reality called God.

In the first part of this book we shall be looking into the glass placed before us by one of the great biblical story-tellers, an otherwise unknown man called Mark. His short work has a narrative order of events; but it is not in my judgement a straightforward one, since words, phrases, symbols and allusions bounce backwards and forwards across the apparently simple story, suggesting deeper layers of meaning and revelation. We shall not therefore go through the Gospel section by section, as in a commentary, but use a pattern which tries to reflect the haunting impression that Mark has made on me. The pattern is at first geographical. In Chapter 1 we shall attend to Mark's scenes in desert and mountain, where the transcendence and otherness of Jesus are accentuated. Chapter 2 moves to his scenes 'by the sea', the place of teaching and encounter and the reversal of ordinary expectations. In Chapter 3 we look at those passages where Jesus is 'in the boat' or 'on the road', with his disciples yet apart from them. Chapter 4 begins with scenes in synagogues and houses, then moves through the Temple of Jerusalem into the more concentrated narrative and symbolism of Mark's account of the passion. The story ends yet does not end at the tomb (Chapter 5), where the absence of Jesus appears to be bound up with a mission to the gentiles.

In a sense all of Mark's readers today are 'gentiles' or outsiders; if we attend at all imaginatively to the Gospel we can hardly avoid being baffled by it. The second part of this book tries to treat that response constructively. How can we seriously listen to these ancient stories, and what practical effect can they have? Is it possible to be disciples of Jesus and to have a Christian lifestyle today? If God is as elusive as he appears to be, what place is left for the Church's mission and sacraments? It may be that Mark's vision and story of Jesus provide us with some answers, even if they are not very comfortable ones. Nor can they be very neat ones, which is why the pattern of this book gets disrupted, contemporary experience often breaking into the first part and the story of Jesus into the second part. But our starting-point at least is clear: 'the beginning of the good news . . .'.

PART ONE

The Beginning of the Gospel

1 *From the Wilderness*

Many times I have asked people to read right through the Gospel of Mark—reading it as one would a short story, and trying to forget anything that Matthew or Luke or John wrote—and then to come back a week later and say what effect the reading had. Some are mystified, others thrilled, others repelled; most find a mixture of all these reactions inside themselves. And repeatedly there are two things that strike the reader (or better, the listener, for like all the books of the New Testament this one was originally written to be read aloud). The first is the stark, relentless sense of destruction and death that fills particularly the final part of Mark's book but spreads its tentacles back as far as the second chapter. And the other is the blindness and stupidity of Jesus' disciples.

We shall wait a bit before thinking of the death and destruction, though that is hard with the cross looming over the pages of this Gospel. But what of the disciples? The Church calls them 'saints', which makes us suppose they should be filled with holiness, virtue and wisdom. And the Christian likes to imagine that those who knew Jesus in the flesh were especially privileged and enlightened, people who could say with the confidence of a later book of the New Testament, 'That which was from the beginning, which we have heard, which we have seen with our eyes, which we have looked upon and touched with our hands, concerning the word of life . . . that which we have seen and heard we proclaim also to you' (1 John 1.1–3). But in Mark's dull and frightened men there is little sign of that confidence. Matthew, Luke and John all tone down their numb stupidity, but none of them can eradicate the impression of fumbling mortals trying vainly to cope with the invasion of their little world by divine glory and terror. They—and we, if we read their story with openness and imagination—are plunged into a new world that makes us shudder yet will not let us go; a world that opens our eyes but perplexes them, driving later writers to talk of 'dazzling darkness' and 'radiant obscurity'; a world dominated by a man who showers us with acts and words of power but who is himself bound and beaten by the established powers of the old world.

Think how this man appears on the scene. St Mark has no inspiring tale of Jesus' conception and birth to begin his book, as has St Luke, no impressive genealogy like St Matthew's, no homage to the eternal Word like St John's. 'The beginning of the good news', he says; he quotes the prophet Isaiah's saying about God's messenger crying in the wilderness; and immediately we are in that wilderness and Isaiah's words are fulfilled by the sudden appearance of a wild man. Mark does not tell us where John the Baptist comes from, though later in his book we hear more of his mission and his end. All that matters now is that this man of the desert, with his camel-hair clothing and his diet of locusts and wild honey, is preparing for a wilder, stronger one to come. And by the ninth verse of the book, there he is, being baptized: 'and in those days Jesus came from Nazareth of Galilee'. That is all we are told of Jesus' earthly origins, though Mark will tell us later that his family thought he was mad (3.21) and that the people of his home town had little time for him (6.1–6). In a sense Nazareth is of no consequence, for in the very next verse we read, 'immediately he saw the skies torn apart and the Spirit like a dove descending upon him, and there was a voice from the skies, "You are my son the beloved; with you I am well pleased".' It is similar to the irony in the fourth Gospel: this man is not really 'from Nazareth', he is from God. He is filled with the Spirit, he and he alone according to Mark. The disciples do not receive the Spirit, not even the twelve who are appointed to be 'with Jesus' (3.14), and there is no evidence that they or even John the Baptist were aware of this revelation at the River Jordan. It belongs to the secret knowledge Mark shares with his readers.

We are perhaps beginning to see how in this spare story, as in a poem, almost every word counts, even the words that are missed out. There are still some who think of Mark as a clumsy, artless writer or as someone who just made a scrapbook of stories about Jesus and stuck an account of his death on the end. But the more we listen to what he says, putting to one side the imaginative alterations and additions of Matthew, Luke and John and the rather less imaginative theories of form criticism, the more we simply attend to this book as Scripture and therefore as literature: then the more we are likely to be held by the pace of its story-telling, by the tautness of its structure and by the way its words and symbols echo back and forth over the man from Nazareth who is the Son of God, making some sense of his life and death, but more importantly urging *us* to make sense of them in our own lives and deaths. But first we must recognize that our 'common' sense is in fact non-sense and that it is in the non-sense of the crucified Messiah that we must discover the sense of God. Mark is putting into story form the same paradox that St Paul impressed on the Christians of Corinth, and with the same urgency: 'Jews demand signs and Greeks seek wisdom, but we preach Christ crucified, a stumbling-block to Jews and folly to gentiles, but to those who are called, both Jews and Greeks, Christ the power of God and the wisdom of God. For the foolishness of God is wiser than men, and the weakness of God is stronger than men' (1 Cor. 1.22–5).

Now one of the ways Mark uses words and symbols to reveal the dazzling darkness of the Son of God is by his sense of place. Many readers have responded to the contrast this Gospel draws between Galilee and Jerusalem: in both there is conflict and hostility to Jesus, but while Galilee is the place of preaching and of mission, Jerusalem (where he goes only in the last week) is the place of destruction. In Galilee Jesus is unbound, in Jerusalem he is bound: in Jerusalem too he breaks the bounds of death and 'goes ahead into Galilee', from which the good news is to reach all nations. This geographical pattern of Jesus' ministry could be historically accurate, though Luke and John change it out of all recognition: the important point is the *symbolic* sense. Again Mark is expressing in story what Paul tries to convey in his arguments about Law and circumcision and righteousness and faith: that with Jesus a new reality and a new freedom have entered the world and that the old exclusive Judaism is doomed.

17

But 'Galilee' and 'Jerusalem' are not the only symbols of place Mark uses. There is a deliberate pattern in the movement of Jesus between desert and mountain, synagogue and house, boat and road, temple and tombs. So after the irruption of Jesus into the world and the irruption of the Spirit and the voice at his baptism, Mark tells us, 'And immediately the Spirit casts him out into the wilderness. And he was in the wilderness forty days being tested by Satan, and he was with the beasts, and the angels served him.' The echo of Israel's forty years' testing in the wilderness is unmistakable, as it will be later in the 'desert' or 'lonely place' where twice Jesus feeds the lost and hungry people as God had through Moses. Again, twice in the first chapter Mark shows us Jesus trying unsuccessfully to leave human company and to rest in 'deserted places' (1.35, 45; the Greek word is the same in all five instances). The desert is where the good news begins, and however much Jesus is barricaded by crowds and enclosed by walls and bound by his enemies he remains apart from the human world, the one who companies with beasts and angels. We want a man of the fireside or the pub or the family service; but we are met by a man of the wilderness.

This is not to suggest that Mark in any way discredits the full humanity of Jesus or that, as in much of later Christianity, his 'Jesus' is really a god or demigod who puts on human flesh like a cloak. Because the other three Gospels (together with those later Gospels not approved by the Church as Scripture) often heighten the miraculous effect that Jesus has and often remove signs of his human nature that appear in Mark—tiredness, ignorance, anger and so on—it is sometimes said that Mark has, in the theologians' language, a 'low Christology'. But if the sense of Jesus' strangeness and transcendence is anything to go by, then Mark's Christology is 'higher' than Matthew's or Luke's. His is the Gospel where constantly people are amazed and perplexed at the words and deeds of Jesus and where the distance between him and other human beings is widest. For in all the others there are scenes of intimacy between Jesus and his disciples or companions; in Mark's such scenes are rare, fleeting, fraught with conflict and mystery. And this distance is not just a horizontal one, so to speak, with Jesus on the fringe of human society. It is a vertical one too, Jesus being set 'above' the rest of the world, which is what makes his eventual binding and destruction so terrifyingly ironic. He comes from the desert; but he is also the man of the mountains.

In the Old Testament it was in the desert that the people discovered their identity and were confronted with the Way of their strange God. But the mountain was the place where God was worshipped and encountered; the place of revelation (Mount Sinai), the place of sacrifice (Mount Zion), the place of judgement (Mount Carmel). So in Mark's Gospel, after the five thousand had been fed in the wilderness, Jesus dismissed the disciples and the crowd and 'went away to the mountains to pray', just as before he had gone away to pray in a deserted place. But on those earlier occasions in the desert, disciples and crowd can pursue him in their hunger for healing and teaching and bread (1.36; 6.33). To the mountain, however, Jesus goes alone; others can accompany him by invitation only. This happens at two pivotal points in the book. First, after the scene by the sea when—as at the foot of Mount Sinai—representatives of all Israel are gathered, we read that 'he went up on the mountain and called those whom he desired' (3.13; compare Exod. 24.1f.). It is here on the mountain that the Twelve, representatives of the new Israel, are appointed. Mark emphasizes that this is by Jesus' own initiative; the Son of God himself calls the Twelve to come up, for Jesus, unlike even the great Moses, is at home in the mountain, he has been given the Spirit and authority of God, he can boldly enter the cloud that is the presence of the invisible God.

This is even clearer on the second occasion. This time only three are called, 'and he led them up a high mountain apart by themselves'. Here they actually see Moses, but first is mentioned the prophet Elijah. For if the mountain in chapter 3 is a Sinai this one in chapter 9 is also a Carmel, the place where the prophets of the false god Baal were put to rout and the true God of Elijah revealed his power. So as Jesus is transfigured and the terrified Peter babbles on about making shelters or shrines for the three worthies, 'a cloud came over-shadowing them'. The cloud is the *shekinah*: in it is 'the appearance of the likeness of the glory of the Lord', as another prophet, Ezekiel, had described it in awe at the transcendence and otherness of God (Ezek. 1.28; compare Exod. 24.15ff.). From the cloud speaks the voice of God himself. 'And suddenly looking around they no longer saw anybody but Jesus alone with them', for Moses and Elijah belong to the past (as Jesus explains to the three as they descend the mountain) whereas Jesus himself remains to lead the new Israel through its desert of destruction.

There is still one more 'mountain' for Jesus to climb: the Mount of Olives opposite Jerusalem, from which in chapter 13 he prophesies the destruction of Mount Zion where the forces of the old order are gathering to destroy him. There too the authority of Jesus is inescapable: he the victim sits in judgement. In the tension between our lust for power and our fear of freedom, most of us secretly want a leader whom we can simultaneously worship and manipulate. But by now it is plain to the disciples that Jesus is no such leader. When Peter had tried to steer him on to a more comfortable path Jesus had rounded on him, saying, 'You are not thinking the way of God but of men' (8.33). And the attentive reader or listener is prepared for this intransigent authority of Jesus, since he has been told in the title of the book that it is 'the good news of Jesus Christ *the son of God*' and already the heavenly voice has confirmed this. By that title Mark does not mean all that the Church later came to formulate in the doctrine of the Trinity. 'Son of God' does not of itself imply equality with God: in the Old Testament the all-too-human King David was given the same title, whose central association is perhaps with obedience to the Father. But Jesus is greater than David (Mark 12.35–7); indeed, the doctrine of the Trinity is there in germ at Jesus' baptism, when Mark shows the Spirit descending on Jesus whom God declares his beloved Son.

So the wild man of the desert and the mountain is in a unique relationship with God. Each time Mark has the heavenly voice declaring that Jesus is Son of God it is as he is lifted up. The voice speaks at his baptism 'as he was coming up out of the water'; it speaks again at his transfiguration 'on a high mountain'. And there is a third occasion too. When Jesus' authority is shattered and with it is shattered any likeness to a king, let alone a god, when he is lifted up on the cross, the voice speaks once more:

'Truly this was the Son of God'. It is the voice of divine witness again, yet it speaks not from heaven but through the mouth of the soldier supervising the execution. The Greek sentence is ambiguous and has no punctuation, so on a human level it can be read in several ways. Perhaps the centurion was incredulously questioning, 'Was *this man* really the Son of God?'; perhaps he was viciously mocking, 'Some "Son of God" this fellow!'; perhaps he was indeed confessing in faith, 'Truly this *was* the Son of God'.

> I was a stranger, could not read these people
> Or this outlandish deity. Did a God
> Indeed in dying cross my life that day
> By chance, he on his road and I on mine?[1]

The ambiguity on the human level may be deliberate, but on the deeper level Mark's meaning is plain: the voice as before is from God, and declares that even here, lifted up now on the cross as before above the water and on the mountain, this man possessed the authority and shared the glory of God, he was the Son of God. 'Was'; whether this 'Son of God' has any future Mark has still to tell us, though he has thrown out some hints.

Now these occasions are not in fact the only times in this Gospel that Jesus is hailed as 'Son of God'. On his first visit to a synagogue recorded by Mark, a man with an unclean spirit cries out, 'What have you to do with us, Jesus of Nazareth? Have you come to destroy us? I know who you are, the Holy One of God.' We have difficulty today in conceiving of the reality of 'unclean spirits'—not that demonic power is any less threatening in our century, simply that we describe it in more scientific ways. But whether biological, psychological or sociological, it still needs exorcism, that is, the chastity and courage to penetrate to the root of the evil, name it and confront it with the authoritative voice of healing; and now as then when the 'evil spirit' meets that purgative fire it is likely to squirm and resist. (So we talk of the 'fight' put up by cancerous cells; or we might think of the resistance of our psyche to the invasive power of human love, or of the residual conscience of the self-indulgent rich justifying themselves in the face of poverty.) Not only for St Mark but for the

21

first Christian millennium, however, this conflict was seen as one between supernatural spirits, and the work of the Spirit-filled Christ as one of victory over the demons or Satan. And the demons were seen as possessing spiritual sight. So Mark shows the unclean spirit recognizing the fire of judgement that in Jesus has entered the synagogue. Even more explicitly, at the symbolic scene of 'all Israel' gathered on the shore before Jesus appoints the Twelve, 'whenever the unclean spirits saw him they fell down before him and screamed out, "You are the Son of God"' (3.11).

But though they recognize the Son of God, this spiritual sight is like the faith of the demons in the Letter of James who 'believe and shudder' (Jas. 2.19). For Mark faith involves more than sight or knowledge, it involves the readiness to hear good news and to lose life. That is made plain to Peter after he has confessed Jesus as the Messiah but immediately shown that he does not wish himself or his Messiah to face the destructive power that threatens them. And it is plain too in the strange story of the madman possessed by 'Legion'. Again the spirits hail Jesus, this time as 'Son of the Most High God' (a gentile title, for this is gentile territory), but after they have been dramatically expelled the man is sent by Jesus to tell his people of God's goodness to him. He goes off to 'proclaim in the Decapolis how much Jesus had done for him' (the word *kērussein* is the early Church's technical term for preaching the gospel): and it is only at this point that faith in Mark's sense enters the story. Unfortunately it is not only among demons and not only in the first century that spiritual sight can be unaccompanied by responsive faith.

There are other telling details in the story of the madman. When after their comical bargaining session with Jesus the unclean spirits are expelled they enter the pigs—fittingly, since for the Jews pigs are themselves unclean—and the pigs rush down the cliff and drown in the sea. This is even more fitting, for the sea is the haunt of demons, the ungovernable primal chaos. Yet even here Jesus is the governor. On the way to the madman's haunts he has calmed the storm that threatened to sink the boat, using the same word of exorcism that had earlier cast out the unclean spirit in the synagogue. 'Who then is this, that even wind and sea obey him?' ask the terrified disciples, for such power is the prerogative of God,

> who dost still the roaring of the seas,
> the roaring of their waves and the tumult of the peoples
> (Psalm 65.7).

The 'sea' that Jesus calms is in fact the Lake of Galilee, which can be stormy enough but is hardly an ocean. Luke refers to it more correctly as a 'lake', but for Mark it is always 'the sea', since again it is the symbolic sense that counts. The vanquisher of demons, the man of the desert and of the mountains, is lord also of the sea. Later the disciples even see him walking on its water, while at the beginning of his teaching in parables he 'got in a boat and sat on the sea' (to translate literally the Greek of Mark 4.1; this echoes the praise of God in Psalm 29:

> The Lord sits enthroned over the flood:
> the Lord sits enthroned as King for ever.)

Repeatedly, by his subtle use of symbolic words and settings, Mark shows the divine authority that this Jesus wields, and repeatedly he records the amazement, awe and terror of the men and women who come near him. So the terror is all the harsher when from chapter 8 this lord of sea and mountain, referring to himself as 'the Son of Man', begins to talk openly of a humiliating death he must undergo; the irony all the crueller when at the end he is bound and killed and no single shaft of light pierces the demonic scene of spite and agony and the so-called Son of God cries out, 'My God, my God, why hast thou forsaken me?', and no one in heaven or earth comes to his aid. Few writers in all history have ever conveyed so palpable a sense of mockery and *Schadenfreude* as does Mark in his gaunt account of the conviction and execution of Jesus.

Now it is just before this tide of mockery engulfs the master of the sea that we hear him for the only time in the Gospel accepting the titles that have been bestowed on him by the heavenly voice, by Simon Peter and by the demons. On previous occasions, when Jesus was radiant with authority, those who had experienced the revelation of Jesus as Messiah or Son of God were told to keep it

23

secret (3.12; 8.30; 9.9). But now he is bound and silent as false accusations rain around him. Then the high priest puts a straight question to him, combining the two titles that the reader has already heard given to Jesus: 'Are you the Messiah, the Son of the Blessed?' The question is riddled with ambiguity, for Mark habitually uses few adjectives or adverbs and scarcely ever gives us direct insight into a person's thoughts or feelings. It is up to us to conjecture the tone and underlying meaning of the high priest's question; or if we will we can interpret it not as a question but as an inspired statement like the earlier shouts of the unclean spirits and the later 'confession' of the centurion (for Mark as for the Old Testament, the Spirit of God is indiscriminate in the mouthpieces it chooses). And the irony is compounded by Jesus' reply: 'I am, and you shall see the Son of Man seated on the right hand of the Power and coming with the clouds of heaven.' Now that he is shorn of all external authority and glory, Jesus accepts the titles, but he then refers to himself as 'Son of Man' (the only status he has previously claimed), the redeeming Lord of Daniel's vision who will come on the clouds of heaven. The statement is preposterous. This man is a prisoner with no chance of escaping to the next room let alone the clouds of heaven, he is a blasphemer whom God must already have cursed, so that it only remains for the authorities to execute God's judgement on him. Yet of course Mark means all those titles and images to dart around the head of Jesus even while he is led to Pilate and to Golgotha; as they dart around his whole story from the River Jordan to the mountain of glory, from the screams of the demons to the confession of Peter, from the title of the book to the final ambiguous judgement of the centurion; as they dart around the reader's head, whipping up the intolerable tension between the exaltation and the degradation of Jesus. In the end there are only two ways of mitigating the tension: either we throw the book away in despair and opt for a gentler religion, or we act upon it and attempt to follow this man through glory and through terror.

We can see the whole of Mark's book as constituting this invitation and this warning. And although so much of the teaching is indirect and 'in parables', at the very centre of the book is the direct call to the reader, 'If anybody wishes to come after me,

24

let him deny himself and take up his cross and follow me. For whoever wishes to save his life will lose it; and whoever loses his life for my sake and the gospel's will save it ...' (8.34f.). The words are interpreted within Mark's story both by the prediction of Jesus' suffering and the rebuke to Peter which precede them and by the transfiguration which follows them; but they are put there above all to be interpreted *outside* the written story in the stories of the readers' own lives and deaths. Mark is asking us to throw away our fascination with our identity and titles as Jesus threw his away on the mockery of the Sanhedrin and the soldiers; he is asking us to abandon that desperate religious search for 'personal salvation' which perhaps led us to read his book in the first place. He is a cruel and uncompromising writer, and it is not surprising that his successors in the craft of Gospel-writing tried to lower the tension. Matthew, Luke, John and later writers and thinkers have insights and skills that Mark did not possess; but nowhere again shall we find in such troubling narrative form that identity of the transcendent lord of the mountain with the degraded and vilified prisoner, an identity maintained even when he reaches what is literally the breaking-point of crucifixion; and nowhere again shall we find such insistence that for all the sombre power of this story it is not ultimately by contemplating it but by entering it that we begin to make sense of it. And entering the story means allowing ourselves to be pulled out of the story, drawn by the same Jesus who in the end leaves the story with the promise that he 'goes ahead'. And that in turn means accepting the terrifying wildness and authority of Mark's Jesus. It is after all a Gospel we are dealing with, not a biography or a theological meditation or a compendium of wise moral teaching.

This book then was written for practical and pastoral purposes, as indeed were all the writings of the New Testament. Assuming that Mark's was the first 'Gospel' to be written, its form inspired at least three other imitators or adaptors, and Matthew in particular keeps quite close to Mark in the outline and vocabulary of his book. Yet in many ways the New Testament writer closest to him in spirit and literary approach is not the didactic Matthew but the prophetic John of Patmos. The Book of Revelation uses as its framework a mass of traditional symbols which it interprets through an elusive story. Mark on the other hand uses as its framework a straightforward story which it interprets through an echoing forest of symbols. Permeating these two uncompromising and mysterious books are the overwhelming sense of the authority of Jesus both in his glory and in his destruction and equally the conviction that the reader must become or remain a disciple and undergo the same destruction of his or her earthly identity and status. The writer of the Apocalypse adapts a by then conventional Jewish literary form to encourage his Christian readers in the face of persecution. Mark goes one step further and invents a new form. Whether he realized it or not, the writing of the first Gospel was a revolutionary act. It involved an even more definite break with the religious past than Paul's disputes, for a new story is more powerful, more universal and more communicable than a new argument. The story of Jesus was written to replace the story of the Exodus.

Yet clearly Mark treats the Old Testament (including the Exodus) as Scripture and depends heavily on it for his style of narrative, just as Paul does for his arguments and the seer of the Apocalypse for his images. The literary critics Erich Auerbach and Robert Alter have both emphasized the 'laconic' style of the Old Testament, seeing it not as a primitive naivety but as an artistic subtlety bound up with the Hebrew belief in an elusive and invisible God. So Auerbach contrasts Homer's account of the origin of Odysseus' scar, where outward appearance and inner thoughts are fully described and all is 'foreground', with the account in Genesis of Abraham's binding of his son Isaac, a sparse narrative 'fraught with background'. In the latter, thoughts and feelings and appearances are not mentioned; adjectives and adverbs hardly occur; all we have is a brief story and some dialogue. There are no spare words: without becoming conventionally 'poetic', prose is heightened. And so it is with the parables of Jesus and with the whole parable of Jesus himself told by Mark. The meaning is not in the foreground, it is far back in the narrative. As with the fourth Gospel, there is constant irony between the surface meaning of the words and their elusive real meaning. Yet John is kinder to us: he puts his 'real' meaning in the mouth of Jesus, however hard it is to accept, whereas Mark still conceals his in parables and images and in the final apparently pointless degradation of Jesus, so that his readers must work and hunt as well as listen. Then, as we hunt, the words of Mark's Jesus to his disciples leap out at us: 'Do you still not understand?' And with them we must furtively answer 'No', and continue with the search.

Note

1 Edwin Muir, 'The Killing', *Collected Poems*, Faber 1964.

2 *Inside Out*

As we hunt for the meaning of this story and through it for what Mark calls 'the mystery of the kingdom of God', we are given companions. These are the disciples, the learners, the ones who follow Jesus, with whom Christian readers at any rate will tend to identify themselves. So it is important to find out where their discipleship begins.

Most people have a vague picture of Jesus wandering around Galilee teaching, and saying to all and sundry, 'Follow me'. In fact this is not shown happening in any of the four Gospels. Although Mark frequently depicts Jesus surrounded by crowds and with an inchoate group of disciples, he has only five instances of people being 'called', whereas there are at least eleven occasions when Jesus tells people to go away. These five are: the calling of Simon and Andrew, then of James and John, in the first chapter; the calling of Levi the tax-collector a little later; the calling of the Twelve 'up the mountain' where they are appointed as companions, evangelists and exorcists; and the calling of the rich man in chapter 10. With the exception of this last unsuccessful invitation to follow, which happens in Judea or Trans-Jordan 'as Jesus was setting out on his way', all of the calls take place 'by the sea', that is, on the shore of the Sea of Galilee. (The call of Levi, to be precise, takes place as Jesus leaves the shore; presumably a tax office would not actually be sited on a beach, but the account of his call is clearly a part of the same scene as Jesus' teaching by the sea in the previous verse.) By now we should be accustomed enough to Mark's symbolic use of places to know that this repetition of 'by the sea' is more than an historial reminiscence, though doubtless it is that too. The shore, where the 'gospel' is proclaimed and where its adherents are called, is the boundary between the human world of land, the ordered life of town and country, of business and religion, of seeds and lamps and vineyards, and the demonic world of sea, the lawless haunt of monsters, storms and destructive depth.

This is not fanciful, but answers to a sense of place rooted in human experience. Even today, when nature on land and sea is so expertly managed, we think of 'dry land' as a place of sense and security and of the sea as a place of mystery and danger. Every night countless people undergo nightmares of drowning. Seafarers—such as Jesus' first disciples were in their small way— still belong to an uncanny sub-culture, and the leviathans or creatures of the sea are far more sinister to us than any tiger. Even though the modern 'seaside' is frequently cluttered with caravans and ice-cream stalls, the sense of boundary retains its power, as anyone seeing the sea for the first time or standing for long upon a cliff-top can testify. This is where firmness and order and civilization end, and all that lies ahead is random and meaningless, even on the almost tideless Mediterranean or the little Sea of Galilee. And the point that Mark seems to be making in his episodes 'by the sea' is that if we want to receive the mystery of the Kingdom of God we must go to that boundary. It is natural for us to want a way of salvation that begins unambiguously in our familiar city or village without disturbing its settled life. Some brave souls, on the other hand, maintain that to find the way we must go 'out of the world', whether into fiery asceticism or into an esoteric fantasy-world or into the vast depths of the individual psyche. But the shore is neither the one nor the other, neither the solid world of ordered society nor the watery expanse of existential dread, though it partakes of both. And this is where Mark's crowd must go in search of its God, this is where its members may be called to follow the Son of God.

Now the word 'disciple' implies both following and learning. To be a disciple in Mark's sense requires not only a release from human attachments and possessions to follow a new way of life but also a release from conventional attitudes and concepts to *understand* in a new way, to discover the mystery of God's Kingdom or rule. So the shore is the place of teaching as well as of calling. After the forgiveness and healing of the paralysed man, and just before the call of Levi, Jesus 'went out again by the sea, and all the crowd came to him, and he taught them' (2.13). 'All the crowd' becomes even vaster in chapter 3 just before the appointment of the Twelve, where, as we saw earlier, the 'great multitude' represents all Israel, 'from Galilee and Judea and Idumea and Trans-Jordan and from about Tyre and Sidon'; so great that a boat has to be got ready for Jesus in case the crowd crushes him. This actually happens the next time Jesus teaches by the sea; Mark stresses that the crowd is 'by the sea on the land' while its teacher is 'in a boat on the sea'. In this boundary setting, carefully crafted in so few words, the teaching begins. And it too is a teaching of the boundary, 'in parables', where the listener is constantly struggling between carnal and spiritual meaning.

'Listen', says Jesus. This is to be the declaration of God's Word to his people, echoing the *Sh'ma*, 'Hear, O Israel . . .', that they recite daily. God's Spirit-filled teacher is seated in authority in the boat, as later he will sit in authoritative judgement over the religious establishment of Jerusalem on the colt, in the Temple and on the Mount of Olives. But the words that follow in the story of the sower, the supposedly 'simple teaching' of parables, have been argued over by preachers and interpreters ever since. What *is* it that is kept secret and then made manifest? What *is* this Kingdom of God that is like a seed growing from insignificance to give shelter to the birds of the air? It should not surprise us that interpretation of these riddles still goes round in circles, for according to Mark the teaching failed the first time it was given, like a joke at which nobody laughs. 'Those about him with the twelve', the ones who should be expected to grasp the teaching, asked for an explanation. But by the time a joke has been laboriously explained it has lost its point; and so it is, many people have felt, with Mark's interpretation of the parable of the sower (4.14–20). Yet perhaps that is the point, that it has no point. For according to Mark the parables *conceal* the mystery (or secret) of the Kingdom of God, which is given to the disciples and promptly lost by them. They are about God, the hidden God of Israel who speaks to his people but who cannot be put into words or encapsulated in 'points'. Therefore they do not mention God. The word 'God' hardly ever occurs in Jesus' teaching in Mark, except in the phrase 'the kingdom of God', and only once (at 12.27) is it the subject of a sentence he utters. Christians, so eager to celebrate the arrival of God's Kingdom, have often been impatient with this blend of elusiveness and reverence and prodigal in their talk of God; whereas Judaism, deeply suspicious of idolatry and therefore of theology, is still more at home with teaching 'in parables'.

Now this is very frustrating, for those disciples and for us. Mark's book is supposed to be 'good news', and Jesus begins his preaching by saying, 'the time is fulfilled, and the kingdom of God is at hand'. He talks of people 'receiving' and 'entering' the Kingdom (9.47; 10.15, 23ff.); of its belonging to children (10.14); he tells a scribe that he is 'not far from' the Kingdom (12.34); and even says to his disciples that some of them will 'see' it coming in power (9.1). Again, two of those parables in chapter 4 begin encouragingly, 'the kingdom of God is like . . .' (4.26, 31). Surely the nearness of this Kingdom, that can be sought, received, entered, owned and depicted, means that God himself is near, that meaning is possible and that we can cross the fence of the parable. Or at least that some of us can, those insiders to whom 'has been given the secret of the kingdom of God'. But the insiders stumble and fall away, and in the end the secret or mystery is whittled down to a man forsaken by God, a king with no kingdom. So perhaps *this* is the point, that the disciples cannot grasp the mystery of the Kingdom because the mystery is Jesus himself, whom they cannot hold or follow. The puzzling words that Jesus says to his disciples after the parable of the sower, 'to you the mystery has been given of the kingdom of God', were altered by Matthew and Luke to read, 'to you it has been given *to know* the *mysteries* of the kingdom of God/heaven', which is altogether less frustrating and more in tune with normal religious expectation. With Matthew and Luke as our tutors we can work away at these sayings, parables and events one at a time, confident that we are familiarizing ourselves with the mysteries and coming closer to the Kingdom of God. But in Mark it is all or nothing, *the* mystery of Jesus that attracts and repels and that resists understanding and control because it is not conceptual or verbal but personal. There is much hard teaching in Matthew's Sermon on the Mount and in Luke's powerful parables, but nothing

31

like what Frank Kermode calls the 'gloomy ferocity' of Mark chapter 4.

The ferocity is at its height in the rest of the sentence just quoted (Mark 4.11f.), which Matthew and Luke again soften substantially and over which many gallons of twentieth-century ink have been spilt. The sentence reads in full, 'To you the secret (or mystery) has been given of the kingdom of God; but to those outside everything is in parables, so that seeing they may see and not perceive, and hearing they may hear and not understand, lest they should turn again and be forgiven.' This seems intolerable to us. The apparent élitism of the contrast between 'those about Jesus' and 'those outside' offends the modern conscience. So does the apparent belief in predestination and the idea that God should *not* want some people to repent and be forgiven. From Matthew and Luke onwards, all sorts of ingenious solutions have been worked out to show that Mark could not possibly have meant this, let alone Jesus. Yet the words about seeing and hearing, which are quoted from the vision and call of Isaiah (Isa. 6.9f.), expressed vividly the old prophets' sense of their word (which was God's Word) being rejected by their dull and self-indulgent audiences; and Mark shows the prophet Jesus experiencing the same rejection. His parables, like those of Amos and Ezekiel, are met with incomprehension and hostility, and in the end it is after the plainest parable of them all, that of the vineyard, that the serious attempt to arrest him begins. He is killed by his own words; yet, Mark tells us, they are words that 'will not pass away' (13.31), they are *the* Word (2.2; 4.33).

For Mark, as in the Old Testament, the Word of God judges and divides, 'living and active, sharper than any two-edged sword, piercing to the division of soul and spirit, of joints and marrow, and discerning the thoughts and intentions of the heart' (Heb. 4.12). The Word takes hold of the prophet and through him addresses the people from outside, so to speak, like the new cloth and new wine of Jesus' parables in chapter 2, like Jesus himself coming from the wilderness. So in a way the parables both are *about* the Word and *are* the Word; or we could say that Jesus himself is the parable—and later on John will assert that Jesus is the Word. If it truly is the transcendent God who is addressing us in these enigmatic words about seeds and lamps, if for mortal men and women this teaching is an encounter with the hidden God, then such is their distance from God that misperception and misunderstanding are inevitable. In the language of the Bible, the hearers are being judged. But 'judgement' is not—as the last thousand years of Christianity would usually have it—the eternal salvation or damnation of individual souls, a notion which scarcely appears in the New Testament. Judgement is the division that occurs between those who respond and those who do not when human beings encounter ultimate truth and meaning. All this is made explicit, though no less troubling, in the fourth Gospel, where Jesus says 'For judgment I came into this world, that those who do not see may see and that those who see may become blind' (John 9.39), but where he adds that 'the word that I have spoken will be their judge' (12.48) and that in another sense people judge themselves by their 'belief' or lack of belief in Jesus (3.18–20). In both Gospels the judgement hinges on response to the words of Jesus: the cryptic words of the discourses in John, and the even more cryptic words of the parables in Mark.

So it seems that in this response or lack of it a division is made, as in the fourth Gospel, between the Church and 'the world'. Those 'with Jesus', the insiders, are judged righteous, 'those outside' are judged sinners; and if we identify ourselves with the insiders then this judgement is very congenial. Except that we now meet Mark's sharpest reversal of expectation—and possibly the escape from our dilemma if we object to this whole business of division—which is that *everybody* is an outsider. The disciples with their privileged private explanations receive them precisely because they do not understand, and their incomprehension is not diminished but increased as Jesus' teaching continues. Dimly they mumble about bread in the boat and stumble behind Jesus on the road to Jerusalem. With fearful irony Mark has Jesus turn on them the words of Isaiah he had used about the 'outsiders': 'Are your hearts hardened? Having eyes do you not see, and having ears do you not hear?' (8.17f.). As John Drury has shown, the interpretation of the parable of the sower is fulfilled in Mark's own story of the blundering disciples. The seed 'on the road' which Satan snatches away is faithless Peter who 'on the road' rebukes Jesus and is himself rebuked as Satan (4.15; 8.27, 32f.); the seed on the rock which 'falls away' when tribulation comes is the disciples forsaking Jesus and fleeing (4.16f.; 14.50); the seed choked by thorns is the rich man with his desire for life choked by his great possessions (4.18f.; 10.22). But the seed that bears fruit thirtyfold and sixtyfold and a hundredfold is not seen in the story that follows, only hinted at in the future beyond it.

Both the spoken parables of Jesus' teaching and the acted parable of his life amount to a reversal of expectation. The tiny seed becomes a tree for the birds to nest in, the vineyard is given to new tenants; he who loses his life will save it and he who would save it will lose it; the Son of God is a crucified criminal, and the entombed body is not there. And 'many that are first will be last, and the last first'. This final saying (10.31) is placed just before Jesus begins to 'go up to Jerusalem', where its truth will be demonstrated, but it could apply to almost any point in the story. Already in chapter 1 Jesus touches the unclean leper; an outcast tax-collector is called to follow him in chapter 2, after which Jesus shares table fellowship with other such characters, people who should be last. In chapter 3, those who should be first of all in his life, his own family, come to seize him because, they say, 'he's mad' (3.21—this verse is too strong for Matthew and Luke, who both omit it, also toning down Jesus' response later). The word for 'seize' (*kratēsai*) is the same word that is used five times in chapter 14 of the conspirators and soldiers: here is the irony that the first people who try to arrest Jesus are those 'of his own house'. While they are trying to get their message to him, however, Jesus is engaged in argument with the scribes who have accused him of casting out demons in the name of the chief demon. Against them he speaks the parables of the divided house and kingdom and then the words about the unforgivable sin of blaspheming against the Holy Spirit; for, Mark adds in explanation, 'they had said "He has an unclean spirit"'. The scribes have attributed to demonic sources the work of God's Spirit, which we have been told has descended on Jesus; they have in effect called God Satan, no greater blasphemy is conceivable. Well, we know by now from the controversies of the previous chapter that the scribes are the 'baddies' in Mark's Gospel, so though Jesus' words are harsh we think it applies just to them. But at this point Jesus' mother and brothers arrive outside the house, and we realize that they too are implicated, for they had attributed his inspired words and actions to madness. So they have become enemies, they are not let in—literally 'standing outside'—while Jesus says to the insiders, 'those sitting about him', 'Here are my mother and my brothers! Whoever does the will of God is my brother, and sister, and mother.'

It is odd then that one of the main expectations of the Christian Church is that it should uphold 'family life'. There may be excellent reasons for doing so, but we shall not find them in Mark's subversive little book. His Jesus has no such expectations either for himself or for his followers, who are told, 'brother will hand over brother to death, and the father his child, and children will rise up against parents and have them put to death; and you will be hated by all for my name's sake' (13.12f.). We shall hear of Jesus' family just once more, at the beginning of chapter 6 when he comes to Nazareth. There his fellow-citizens, 'insiders' familiar with Jesus, tie him down with a label: 'Isn't this the carpenter, the son of Mary and brother of James and Joses and Simon, and aren't his sisters here with us?' So they can easily dismiss him, and Mark tells us they 'stumbled on him' or 'took offence at him' (the word *skandalizō* is that used by the early Church for those who rejected the gospel). His very humanity and familiarity are the stumbling-block. Again and again we read of people being amazed at Jesus, but here in his home town is the only place where Mark tells us that Jesus himself was amazed, 'because of their lack of faith'. His own people are outsiders, excluded from the mystery of the Kingdom of God.

This expression 'stumbling-block' (*skandalon*) comes from a verse of the prophet Isaiah quoted more than once in the New Testament, where the stone is a metaphor for God: 'The Lord will become a sanctuary, and a stone of offence and a rock of stumbling to both houses of Israel, a trap and a snare to the inhabitants of Jerusalem. And many shall stumble thereon; they shall fall and be broken; they shall be snared and taken' (Isa. 8.14f.). Later in the same book a very different sort of stone is promised by the Word of God:

35

Behold, I am laying in Zion for a foundation
    a stone, a tested stone,
a precious cornerstone, of a sure foundation,
He who believes will not be in haste (in Greek OT
'will not be put to shame') (Isa. 28.16);

while Psalm 118 has a stone transformed:

The stone which the builders rejected has become
    the head of the corner:
This is the Lord's doing,
    and it is marvellous in our eyes.

This last text is the one quoted by Jesus with reference to himself
at the end of the parable of the vineyard in all the first three
Gospels. Elsewhere in the New Testament, all three texts are laid
side by side in the first Letter of Peter (1 Pet. 2.6–8), while Paul
conflates the two from Isaiah in his attempt to understand God's
purposes for Israel and the gentiles (Rom. 9.32f.; compare 1 Cor.
1.23). The verb *skandalizō* ('stumble') is, as we have seen, the one
used of Jesus' fellow-citizens 'taking offence' at him in Nazareth
and of the seed sown in rocky ground which 'falls away' when
tribulation comes. Clearly these texts haunted the early Christians
as they pored over the Jewish Bible searching for intimations
of their Lord. The words stood out because they seemed to
prophesy both the glory and the rejection of the Messiah in his
own life and the mysterious pattern of acceptance and rejection
that met the Church's gospel. Yet according to Mark not only
Jesus' family but the very apostles who are entrusted with preaching are among those who reject the Messiah, as he himself
prophesies on the Mount of Olives: 'You will all stumble.'

Is there anywhere we shall find faith in this book, or does the
parabolic Son of God with his parabolic teaching finally make
everyone an outsider? We saw earlier how the interpretaton of the
parable of the sower is fulfilled in the failure of the disciples; and
Mark's other major parable, that of the vineyard, is also fulfilled,
this time in the death of Jesus that it hastens. But at that fulfilment there is just one person who (if we interpret his words as a
positive statement) responds in faith; that is the outsider, the

gentile centurion. Again, in the whole Gospel there is only one case of a spoken parable received with understanding and wit, and that too is by a gentile, the Greek woman who immediately responds to Jesus' words about throwing the children's bread to the dogs. But these are not completely isolated instances. Throughout the book, as the insiders 'stumble on' Jesus and take offence at him, outsiders also stumble on him and respond with faith. The Twelve, who are specially appointed to be 'with Jesus', forsake him, and one of their number hands him over to his enemies; those to whom he is bound by blood cut themselves off from him; the disciples enclosed with him in the house or the boat have minds that are closed and hardened to his teaching and his way. Yet an 'unclean' woman comes up to him in the crowd and is told that her faith has saved her; insignificant children are placed in the centre and held up as an example; a blind beggar leaps up and follows Jesus on his way. The first are last and the last first, everything is inside out.

In all Mark has twenty-four references to people (other than the disciples, the opponents and 'the crowd') who either encounter Jesus briefly or are seen and referred to by him. They range from very brief appearances like those of Simon of Cyrene and the young man fleeing in the garden to much fuller stories which invite our involvement with the characters, such as the woman with a haemorrhage and the father of the possessed child. And while the insiders are berated for their hardness of heart, many of these outsiders are commended for their faith. When the paralysed man's friends go to all the trouble of removing the roof and lowering the stretcher, Mark tells us that Jesus 'saw their faith'. Bartimaeus, relentlessly crying out for mercy by the road-side, is told 'your faith has saved you', and earlier Jesus had said the same words to the woman who reached out in the crowd to touch his clothes. Immediately after this incident Jairus hears that his daughter has died, and picking up the words he has said to the woman, Jesus tells him, 'Do not fear, only have faith'. 'All things are possible to him who has faith', he says in another scene of despair and confusion; and immediately the possessed boy's father cries out, 'I have faith; help my lack of faith!' In the light of these stories, 'faith' in Mark can perhaps be defined as a persistent reaching out. And we can find the same marks in stories of 'outsiders' where the words 'faith' and 'believe' do not actually occur: the bold approach of the leper in chapter 1, of the deaf and dumb man's friends and of the blind man at Bethsaida. The Syrophoenician woman comes straight to Jesus despite the racial and religious differences, barging into the house where Jesus is trying to lie low. Her daughter is possessed, and she wants exorcism. Jesus is hardly encouraging in the parable he gives her, but she persists with her request and he says, 'for saying this go your way', and the demon is gone: her wit and impertinence are part of faith, and Matthew is following Mark's mind when he has Jesus add, 'O woman, great is your faith.'

Yet a bold and persistent approach is not a presumptuous one. Those in need come forward recognizing the freedom and otherness of Jesus, sometimes falling on their knees, often in considerable anguish, even 'fear and trembling' (5.33); so it is with Jairus, with the woman with the haemorrhage and with the women approaching the supposed place of Jesus' dead body. Again, when Jesus praises children and those with a childlike approach (10.14f.), it is implicitly their faith that he praises: a receptive, persistent, wondering attitude which recognizes the greatness of what is other and does not attempt to manipulate or possess. The contrast with the self-seeking of the official disciples is clear. It is tellingly drawn by Mark in chapter 10, where Jesus puts the same question to two groups of suppliants: 'What do you want me to do for you?' (10.36, 51). From the insiders, James and John, comes the request to sit in state with their Lord; but from the outsider, Bartimaeus the beggar, the simple plea, 'Master, that I may see again'. Yet it is Peter who in the name of the insiders expresses 'faith' in the sense of right belief: 'You are the Christ'. Mark suggests that such faith is inadequate, even irrelevant to discipleship, and subversively shows Jesus commending those who make no confession of faith, those like the children who may be incapable of expressing faith in the conventional sense, those like the widow in the Temple who do not encounter him at all, and those like the unauthorized exorcist who may even have rejected his company (9.38ff.).

We heard Jesus saying to the woman in the crowd, 'Your faith has saved you', and then to Jairus, 'Do not fear, only have faith'; now both these sayings ironically echo his words to the disciples in the boat a few verses earlier, 'Why are you afraid? Have you no faith?' The insiders in this Gospel seem to have the wrong sort of faith, and the outsiders the right sort. Their faith is a warm, human, risky, outgoing movement of their whole lives, like the faith of Abraham that Paul and the writer to the Hebrews point to (Rom. 4; Heb. 11.8–19). It can be contrasted both with the nervous institutional faith of Paul's opponents in Galatia and with the self-indulgent charismatic faith of those in Corinth. Yet we tend to think of 'faith' in one or both of these ways: a Galatian faith, intellectual assent to certain rituals and beliefs, or a Corinthian faith, emotional warmth providing the believer with comfort. So we hear people say, 'he is upholding the faith', or, 'I could never have got through without my faith'. Faith in Mark's sense cannot be an object like the first or a possession like the second: it is something much more dynamic and much more practical than either.

As the Gospel proceeds in its breathless and disturbing way, we begin to see from the 'outsiders' that faith is bound up with generosity. Again there is a contrast with the insiders. The disciples argue about who is the greatest, they ask for places of honour and officiously deter the people bringing children to Jesus. They are pleased with themselves, companions of the mighty Jesus: 'We have left everything and followed you', says Peter. But a little later we shall see a poor widow anonymously putting 'everything she had, her whole living [or life]' into the Temple treasury, just as Jesus is to give his life away (10.45) and as those who would follow him are asked to deny themselves and lose their lives (8.34ff.). Her giving is a crazy extravagance, like that of the other anonymous woman who pours her very valuable ointment over Jesus' head at Bethany. 'Why this waste?' people say, reproaching her. It would be far more just and sensible to sell the stuff and help the poor with the proceeds; but again the riddling Jesus confounds our expectations, warmly commending the wasteful woman and adding that her deed will be recounted all over the world 'wherever the gospel is preached'. By writing his book Mark has ensured that Jesus' words about the woman are

fulfilled; but hearing her story as part of the Gospel we still find it natural to recoil at such prodigal, uncalculating and irrational faith. Significantly, John in his Gospel puts the objections to the woman's action in the mouth of Judas Iscariot: the suggestion is that carping at such out-pourings of generous love is a betrayal of Jesus.

Now perhaps this leads us on to more familiar ground. For surely the good news of Jesus is about love: the love of God for sinners, the compassion of Jesus for those in need, the love of Christians for God and for one another. And certainly the fourth Gospel contains many sayings about the love of God for the world and the mutual love of Christ's disciples. Encouraged also by Luke, we like to see Jesus' healings as acts of compassionate love. And of course there is truth in all this. Yet it is curious that while there are many references to Jesus' anger and indignation there is only one place in all the first three Gospels where he is recorded as loving somebody—and that person is the rich man, who is promptly commanded to give everything away to the poor and follow Jesus (Mark 10.21). Mark does also say that Jesus 'had compassion' on the crowds before each of the meals in the wilderness, but the stress in all four Gospels in recounting these miracles is on their symbolic representation of Jesus' authority (and of the Eucharist and the mission of the Church) rather than on his love for the crowds. (The Greek word for 'showing compassion' also occurs in some versions of the Gospel at 1.41 [the healing of the leper], but scholars are almost unanimous in saying that the correct and original text is 'moved with *anger*'. The noun 'love' does not occur in the whole book.)

In so far as the gospel *is* about love, then, this love of Jesus is clearly a dangerous love, hardly the sort we want to bask in. Indeed, the word 'love' has become so debased that it might be healthy for the Church to declare a moratorium on its use. We may if we wish interpret the mystery of the Kingdom of God that is proclaimed on the shore of the sea as the mystery of God's love; but only, following Mark, if we recognize that it is a fiery love that repels as powerfully as it attracts, one that may call on the beloved to give away all his possessions.

and one said
speak to us of love
and the preacher opened
his mouth and the word God
fell out so they tried
again to speak to us
of God then but the preacher
was silent reaching
his arms out but the little
children the ones with
big bellies and bow
legs that were like
a razor shell
were too weak to come[1]

To hear Jesus speaking the Word of God, people must go to the boundary between order and chaos to face riddles and reversals, and the one who teaches there is less a lover than a stumbling-block.

Now a block or stone is not a thing easily shifted. Despite the attempts to assimilate the Christ in schemes of metaphysics, mysticism, dogma, sacraments, politics, psychology and church order, the Lord of the Gospels still stands on the shore with his call and his parables, and men and women still stumble on him. Whether the stumbling leads to a puzzled cursing withdrawal or to an apprehension of the mystery of the Kingdom of God, that is itself part of the mystery. But if the apprehension is there, then, however far an outsider, one has crossed the boundary and may become a disciple—with all the misunderstanding and disruption that involves.

Note

1 R. S. Thomas, 'H'm', *H'm*, Macmillan 1972.

3 *The Boat and the Road*

The heart of an old-fashioned evangelist's appeal used to be the urge to save yourself from the clutches of hell and eternal damnation. We have become rather coy about hell in recent times, and the modern evangelist's appeal is usually less apocalyptic and more domestic. He will often, for instance, give the impression that if you are converted you will have Jesus as your companion, an infallible partner through life. I remember a university mission where the preacher repeatedly said that the great benefit of making a confession of faith was that one would have 'a personal relationship with Christ'. This struck me first as inept, since most students had found or were feverishly seeking personal relationships that were more tangible and more fun than one with Christ. But also as mischievous. For while there have been some Christians who have claimed to experience Jesus as a constant internal presence or as it were sitting on their shoulder, there have been many others, including great saints, mystics and missionaries, who have struggled with faith and doubt in a looming darkness shot through only with occasional flashes of 'this great absence that is like a presence'. For them, Christ is not on tap, so to speak, in a 'personal relationship': he makes few promises and even they are elusive ones. And if Christ or God *is* a discernible presence in that evangelist's sense, one wonders how far this relationship can be called 'faith', as the Bible uses that word. An earlier evangelist, St Mark, is perhaps more subtle and more faith-ful.

We have seen how in his Gospel the insiders become outsiders and outsiders are received and commended by Jesus. Yet the insiders in all their failure do remain outwardly close to Jesus until loyalty to him becomes intolerable. The twelve men whom

Jesus called up the mountain were appointed 'to be with him, and to be sent out to preach and have authority to cast out demons'. Their task as preachers and exorcists begins then with their being 'with Jesus', his companions. Literally your 'companion' is someone who shares bread with you; and that is what we see those twelve 'insiders' doing with Jesus, most significantly at the supper where he identifies their food and drink with his life, which in less than twenty-four hours will be destroyed. Clearly then this is a perilous companionship. It is worth reading more closely the disciples' story from Galilee to Gethsemane to see how far it is possible to be 'with Jesus' according to Mark.

The call of at least some of the disciples takes place 'by the sea', and the appointment of the Twelve 'on the mountain'. But much of their learning, or rather failing to learn, about Jesus and his way takes place in two other symbolic settings, in the boat and on the road. There is a pattern to this which cannot be accidental. Between chapters 4 and 5 the disciples make six journeys in the boat with Jesus, the Greek words for 'boat' occurring nineteen times up to Mark 8.14. But after they land at Bethsaida we shall not read those words again; there is no more sea and no more journeying on it. On the other hand, when Jesus and the disciples leave Bethsaida (8.27), Mark tells us for the first time in the Gospel that they were 'on the road' (or 'way' or 'path', Greek *hodos*), and between then and their arrival at Jerusalem this *hodos* will be mentioned eight times.

Now both in the boat and on the road the atmosphere is one of confusion and fear. Here are the disciples with Jesus, even enclosed with him by the sides of a boat; yet they are apart from him, separated by their dullness and faithlessness. They hear but do not understand, they see but do not perceive. The six journeys in the boat have puzzled generations of readers, who have pored over Mark's text and over maps of Galilee trying to make some historical or geographical sense of them or, if not, to find some literary or symbolic pattern in them. But in a way their meaning is precisely that they are meaningless. The world where they take place is without form and void, and darkness is upon the face of the deep—the formless sea that is always moving but never leads anywhere. That is where the helpless disciples huddle together in

43

their boat, and where in Jesus the Spirit of God moves over the face of the waters (Gen. 1.1f.: Mark 6.48f.). He too enters the boat, and above the sea's chaos the disciples try in vain to make sense of the secretive revelation that has taken place in the parables on the shore and the meals in the desert. There is no meaning, and they are not with him.

But after the final and most mystifying boat journey, 'let there be light': at Bethsaida a blind man sees, first dimly so that men look like trees, then 'everything clearly'. This is a central episode in Mark's Gospel (though Matthew and Luke omit it altogether); after it the sea is left behind, Jesus and his disciples are on the road and he 'speaks the word to them plainly' (8.32). Yet still they do not or will not see, or in so far as they do see at this stage it is with the vision that cannot distinguish men from trees. Their confusion and fear continue but are now of a different kind. In the boat they had been afraid of storm and drowning, astounded at Jesus' power over the elements and perplexed by the meaning of his words and the numerical significance of the loaves. On the road their fear changes into a stunned, half-blind apprehension of what awaits them at Jerusalem; it is not a reaction to external sights and objects but a fear deep inside them instilled by the direction of their journey and by their leader's threefold prediction of the events at its end (e.g. 10.32–4). The journey now is not a meaningless wandering back and forth; it is on dry land, it leads to Jerusalem, and the plain teaching of Jesus is about what is to happen there and how disciples are to follow him. They cannot accept such talk—Peter actually takes Jesus to task for it—and they suppress the fear it engenders by imagining a more glorious outcome to the journey. Their wilful blindness to the real meaning of the 'road' looks all the more absurd as they quarrel about who is the greatest and ask for places of honour with Jesus.

Now that the sides of the boat no longer enclose them the disciples grow further and further from Jesus. Just before the arrival at Bethsaida Mark showed them in the boat discussing with one another Jesus' mysterious saying about leaven and Jesus overhearing them. When they are on the road this happens more and more. Jesus goes ahead, leaving them to stumble behind questioning among themselves. So as Peter, James and John descend the mountain of transfiguration Jesus tells them to keep the vision secret until the Son of Man has risen from the dead, and 'they held the word to themselves, seeking together what "rising from the dead" meant'. At the foot of the mountain, even more apart from Jesus, are the other disciples, helpless in the task of exorcism to which they had been appointed (9.14–18, 28f.). Then all together they travel through Galilee, Jesus trying to keep their presence hidden because again he is giving plain teaching to the disciples about his death and resurrection. But, Mark adds, 'they did not understand the saying and were afraid to ask him' (9.30–2). On the road they show that Jesus' teaching about losing life and saving it has not taken root in them, by discussing which of them is the greatest; but they are dimly conscious of the absurdity of it, for when he asks them what they were talking about they are ashamed to reply (9.33f.). The impression grows of an embarrassed group of men whispering together away from the fierce glory of Jesus, aware of their stupidity and afraid of his rebuke.

Now the 'road' they walk is leading to Jesus' death: throughout this part of the Gospel his predictions have made that plain. But when they reach Trans-Jordan its direction is made explicit and the city's name is mentioned for the first time since they set out. Again Jesus predicts what awaits him in Jerusalem, this time in greater detail and specifically to 'the twelve'. The picture Mark draws is powerful: 'they were on the road going up to Jerusalem, and Jesus was going ahead of them, and they were amazed, and those who followed were afraid' (10.32). It seems from now on that however hard they try the disciples cannot truly 'be with' Jesus; he is and must be the one who 'goes ahead'. Only twice in the Gospel does Mark state that other people 'go ahead' of Jesus; once after the feeding of the five thousand, when for a reason that is not clear 'immediately he made his disciples get into the boat and go ahead of him to the other side' (6.45), and a second time when he rides into Jerusalem and those going ahead as well as those who follow hail him as Messiah (11.9). Is Mark suggesting that it is as a consequence of their going ahead of Jesus rather than behind him that in the first case the disciples end up in fear and misunderstanding in the boat and that in the second case the crowd's cry changes from 'Hosanna!' to 'Crucify him!'? For 'ahead' is the place for Jesus only. The same word *proagō* ('go ahead') is, as we shall see, used in Jesus' prediction after the Last Supper, 'After I am raised up I will go ahead of you into Galilee' (14.28), and the young man at the tomb repeats the saying to the frightened women (16.7). Jesus' 'going ahead' continues beyond the present story into the future, and not even there can the disciple be with Jesus; she or he is literally a follower, one who goes behind.

This distinction between behind and ahead is what Peter is painfully taught in the central scene of the Gospel on the road near Caesarea Philippi. He has in plain language confessed Jesus as Messiah. But there is no praise of Peter as in Matthew's Gospel; rather Jesus tells the disciples to keep this secret and speaks of being Messiah only obliquely by saying that 'the Son of Man must suffer'. This is when Peter protests. Mark writes that he 'took' Jesus (the verb *proslambanomai* has here rather the sense of a policeman taking someone in hand) and began to rebuke him. We are to imagine Peter moving out in front of Jesus to block his path, for Jesus 'turns round and sees' his other disciples, so that he has his back to Peter as he 'rebukes' him (the same word used of Peter himself in the previous verse). Addressing him as Satan (for as in the interpretation of the sower parable, Satan has snatched away the word sown 'on the road') Jesus says, 'Get back behind me'. 'Behind' is the place for the true disciple, who cannot go ahead of Jesus or remain with him. It was the same word Jesus had used when he first encountered Peter and his brother (literally 'come behind me'), and just after that Mark had added that James and John 'went off behind' Jesus. In case there should be any doubt about this, the same word *opisō* is used in the very next verse, when Jesus says to the disciples and the whole crowd, 'If anyone wishes to follow behind me, let him deny himself and take up his cross and follow me.' Peter is the model of how not to be a disciple: standing in front of Jesus and trying to prevent even him from taking up his cross. Rebuked, he gets back behind Jesus and is indeed the last 'follower' mentioned before the final catastrophe, when after Jesus' arrest he 'followed him from far off' into the high priest's courtyard (14.54). He fails again, but in the young man's message at the tomb there is a hint of restoration and renewed following: 'Go tell his disciples and Peter that he is going ahead of you into Galilee . . .'

In all there are twenty times in Mark's Gospel when we read of people's 'following' or 'going behind' Jesus or being called to do so. It is contrasted not only with 'going ahead of' but also with 'seeking' Jesus. Whenever the word *zēteō* ('seek') appears in Mark it has a negative meaning; it is, for instance, used five times after Jesus' arrival at Jerusalem of his enemies seeking to destroy or arrest him or seeking false evidence. Earlier on, when Jesus is out in the desert praying, the disciples come with the message, 'Everybody's seeking you', and Jesus' response is to go away to other towns (1.35–8). His mother and brothers 'seek' him (3.32) and he is even more abrupt and dismissive, as he is to the Pharisees who 'seek a sign from heaven to test him' (8.11–13). No sign shall be given. The Son of God is not to be sought, he is the free and transcendent one who leads his people. The last characters whom Mark shows 'seeking' Jesus are the women coming to the tomb, and here again the word has a negative meaning, for their search is misconceived: 'You seek Jesus of Nazareth, who was crucified. He has risen, he is not here . . .' The women are looking in the wrong place and in the wrong way, seeking a corpse when they should be following the risen Jesus who goes ahead of them.

'Seeking' in Mark, then, is a movement to grasp and hold and control. Disciples, family, enemies, all attempt this. The 'outsiders' who show faith, on the other hand, approach, as we saw earlier, with a mixture of boldness and fear, recognizing the otherness and authority of Jesus and crying out for mercy or falling on their knees or coming 'in the crowd from behind to touch his cloak' (in the suggestive phrase used of the woman with a haemorrhage). But we also saw earlier that by no means all those who encounter Jesus are called to be followers. Levi and Bartimaeus are shown joining Jesus, even though Bartimaeus was actually told to go away. The restored demoniac who wants to follow his healer is forbidden to; the blind man sent home to stay indoors; the leper, the paralytic and the woman with a haemorrhage all sent home. They have stumbled on the Son of God with faith, and

47

that it seems is enough. For Mark, unlike the more ecclesiastical Matthew and Luke, the purpose of the Church's mission is not really to make disciples but simply to announce the good news. Those who are appointed to the mission call people to repent, they heal and cast out demons (6.7–13): the good news will attract some and repel others, as Jesus did, and if any are called also to be disciples that will be made plain to them, together with the risk it entails.

Through this Gospel runs a missionary tension between preserving the 'mystery' of Jesus and preserving access to him, a tension reflected in the way Jesus is both available and unavailable. For he preaches publicly, he lets the children come to him, he is hemmed in by the crowds; but then he withdraws to deserted places, he tries to remain hidden, he sleeps during the storm, refuses to see people or sends them away. Contact with Jesus is fleeting and unpredictable, and even those called to be with him cannot stay with him; the disciples try to domesticate him as a private possession or cultic object, but he goes ahead and withdraws from them too. At the Last Supper all (including Judas) are together, dipping into the one dish with Jesus and sharing the food and drink which he declares to be his body and blood. But even as they drink the wine he speaks of his not drinking it again until the Kingdom of God comes, and in the episodes that follow on the Mount of Olives and Gethsemane this withdrawal is enacted. He predicts, quoting the prophet Zechariah, that the shepherd will be struck and the sheep scattered, adding the promise that after he is raised up he will go ahead of them to Galilee (Zech. 13.7; Mark 14.27f.). Peter and the others try to contradict the prophecy; they will not fall away or deny Jesus (presumably Judas has already crept off). But before they do fall away there is the sense of Jesus' falling away from them. When they reach Gethsemane he tells all but three of them to 'sit here while I pray'. He withdraws further with Peter, James and John, and then tells them to 'remain here and watch'. Then he withdraws still further to pray. Twice he returns to them and again they withdraw; the disciples in sleep, Jesus in prayer. The third time he returns but now the hour has come, the shepherd is struck and the sheep scattered. He goes ahead bound and they cannot yet follow, though Peter tries to in one last pathetic scene.

There is however one follower we have forgotten. After 'they all forsook him and fled' Mark alone tells us that 'a young man followed him, with nothing but a linen cloth about his body, and they seized him, but he left the linen cloth and ran away naked' (14.51f.). Scholars have conjectured that this mysterious little episode is built on a line from the prophet Amos, 'He who is stout of heart among the mighty shall flee away naked in that day', or on Joseph's fleeing naked from Potiphar's wife (Amos 2.16; Gen. 39). Whether or not there is truth here, we shall soon see that Jesus himself is also to be stripped. Letting oneself be stripped or casting off one's clothes is in fact a symbol of discipleship that runs through the second half of the Gospel. In a detail omitted by Matthew and Luke, Bartimaeus the blind beggar of Jericho 'throws away his cloak' when he is called and runs up to Jesus; after receiving his sight he follows Jesus with the others on the road to Jerusalem. As they enter the city more people tear off their cloaks and throw them on the donkey and on the road. Then on the Mount of Olives the disciples are warned of the coming destruction and told that when it draws near a man who is out in the field is to flee without turning back to take his cloak (13.16); and as Jesus himself is destroyed his clothes are cast away on the gambling soldiers. The whole *motif* of casting off garments is a vivid enactment of what Jesus defines as the requirements of discipleship: 'If anyone wishes to follow behind me, let him deny himself and take up his cross and follow me. For whoever would save his life will lose it; and whoever loses his life for my sake and the gospel's will find it.' The disciple's *psychē*—his life, his identity, his status, his soul, his concern for personal salvation—is to be cast away as one throws off a coat. Nor is this just a 'spiritual' theory. The rich man is called to cast away all his possessions (10.21), and the disciples are warned that their physical life itself may have to be cast off (13.12). In the stripping of the young man in Gethsemane and the stripping of the Son of God at Golgotha is prefigured the practical cost of following Jesus.

If this is so, then it may be that the flight of the young man and the other disciples is not a failure after all but an inevitable part of their being insiders. Certainly Mark sees it as ordained through prophecy, just as are the death of Jesus (14.27) and the deafness and blindness of people to the mystery of the Kingdom of God (4.11f.). Are the disciples blind because they are too close to the dazzling darkness of the Son of God? They are those who eat the body and drink the blood of the shepherd; they have come too near to the mystery and they must be scattered to let him go ahead. The road is impassable until he has been destroyed and passed through death. Three of them had earlier entered the cloud of God's glory with Jesus, but the glory had passed by and Jesus only was left. This glory is the pillar of cloud and fire that went ahead of the Israelites, resting above their camp only for short intervals. It is perhaps hinted at again in the mysterious phrase used of Jesus walking on the water, 'he was going to pass by them' (Mark 6.48), as the glory of God has 'passed by' Moses. When Moses asked to see God's glory he was told to hide in the rock; as the glory passed by, God covered Moses' face with his hand, and only after he has passed by will the Lord remove his hand, 'and you shall see my back, but my face shall not be seen' (Exod. 33.18–23). In his *Life of Moses* St Gregory of Nyssa interprets this strange story as the figure of eternal progress towards God, of the disciple always longing and never satisfied because always being drawn further on; always following and therefore never seeing God face to face since 'he who follows sees the back'. We cannot ask for greater vision: 'to follow God wherever he might lead is to behold God'. So stumbling on the mystery of Jesus and lured on by him, we may be forced to hide in the cleft of the rock or to flee naked from the menacing garden while the terrifying presence of God passes by ahead of us. Genuine contact with the mystery cannot but be fleeting. Jesus' enemies lay hands on him without fear, but he touches people only momentarily to heal or to bless; occasionally an outsider will reach out a hand towards him, if only to catch at his cloak, but the only instance Mark records of an 'insider' touching Jesus is the kiss of Judas. To clutch at Jesus or to claim to possess the truth about him or a personal relationship with him, that is not the way into the mystery. It is a different matter to reckon with the real otherness of the Son of God, and, like Paul, 'forgetting what lies behind and straining forward to what lies ahead . . . press on towards the goal for the prize of the upward call of God in Christ Jesus' (Phil. 3.13f.).

It is perhaps because Jesus is the one who passes by and goes ahead, in the boat and on the road, in the garden and from the tomb, that Mark's narrative has the breathless pace that strikes the most casual reader. 'And . . . and immediately . . . and then . . . immediately . . .' and so on, one event, one saying after another. The word 'immediately' (*euthus* or *eutheōs*) occurs no fewer than 42 times in Mark's short book (38 times in the first 11 chapters, compared with 19 times in Matthew's 28 chapters and seven times in Luke's 24). This has been taken as a sign of the writer's crude style, but is it not rather a natural storyteller's way of conveying the urgency of his story and in particular the urgency of the Christian disciple on his journey after this restless leader? R. S. Thomas writes in his poem 'Pilgrimages':

> There is an island there is no going
> to but in a small boat the way
> the saints went, travelling the gallery
> of the frightened faces of
> the long-drowned, munching the gravel
> of its beaches. So I have gone
> up the salt lane to the building
> with the stone altar and the candles
> gone out, and kneeled and lifted
> my eyes to the furious gargoyle
> of the owl that is like a god
> gone small and resentful. There
> is no body in the stained window
> of the sky now. Am I too late?
> Were they too late also, those
> first pilgrims? He is such a fast
> God, always before us and
> leaving as we arrive . . .[1]

The fast Son of God runs through Mark's fast story and out of it again, leaving behind many riddles, many warnings and some cryptic promises. He 'goes ahead into Galilee'; such is the pace that we cannot catch up with him, and indeed to try to seize him is to become his enemy. For the Christ who can be held and possessed is an idol. The true Son of God for Mark is the one on whom men and women stumble. Dazed by the encounter, some will nevertheless pick themselves up and follow; but even then he is always leading out of our sight, and it is only his back that we can see.

Note

1 From *Frequencies*, Macmillan 1978.

4 The Body Broken

For all the speed and journeying of St Mark's Gospel there are times when Jesus is neither travelling in the boat or on the road nor apart from humanity in the wilderness or on the mountain nor yet on society's boundary 'by the sea'. Several times Mark shows him in a familiar human setting, surrounded by listeners and disciples, enclosed by walls. The walls are those of synagogues and houses.

The Christian movement very early experienced a shift in the setting of its teaching and worship from the synagogue to the house, a shift imposed on it by the opposition of Jewish religious authorities but probably also by the logic of its gospel. As early as the letters of Paul (the fifties of the Christian era) Christian 'house churches' are well established, such as the churches in the houses of Aquila and Prisca, of Nympha and of Philemon (1 Cor. 16.19; Col. 4.15; Philem. 2). Much of the argument of Paul's letters is an interpretation of the leaving of the synagogues and of the emergence of the Christian Church as a movement distinct from though closely allied to Judaism; for Paul's dilemma and his strength was that he experienced so deeply the call of both. We see Paul actually transferring his message from synagogue to house several times in the Acts of the Apostles, and the same shift underlies the harsh attitude to the 'scribes and Pharisees' of St Matthew's Gospel. Mark too is no lover of 'scribes', and in his Gospel the shift is reflected in the setting of Jesus' teaching moving from public synagogue to private house.

The first instance of Jesus' teaching is at Capernaum: 'and immediately on the sabbath he entered the synagogue and taught' (1.21). The congregation is astonished at his authoritative teaching and even more astonished at the authority of his exorcizing.

This begins a pattern of ministry in synagogues that Mark summarizes in the words, 'and he went throughout all Galilee, preaching in their synagogues and casting out demons' (1.39). In chapter 2 controversies and preaching take place in public settings— the shore of the sea, cornfields, houses where crowds gather—but at the beginning of chapter 3 Jesus is again in a synagogue on the sabbath. It is the scene of a tense show of strength between Jesus and 'them' (3.2): the people who watch him looking for an excuse to accuse him are not at this point more closely defined, there is the sense of the whole synagogue as a hostile environment. He calls into the centre the man with a withered hand and throws down the gauntlet to the suspicious congregation: is the sabbath a day for healing and salvation or not? 'But they were silent. And looking round at them in anger, dismayed at the hardness of their hearts, he said to the man, "Stretch out your hand".' It is restored, and the Pharisees go straight from the synagogue to begin plotting how to destroy Jesus.

We shall see Jesus in a synagogue on just one more occasion, his visit to Nazareth (6.1–6, assuming that Nazareth is what is meant by his *patris*). But there he is a stumbling-block, and such is the people's lack of faith that he is unable to do any act of power apart from a few healings. The synagogue, the place where God's Word is to be spoken, has become the place of faithless incomprehension and rebellion against the one who speaks that Word; and we shall not hear of it again except as the place where scribes like to have the best seats (12.39) and where Christian disciples will be beaten (13.9). But immediately after the episode at Nazareth Jesus sends the Twelve out to preach. The instructions about clothing and equipment are precise, as are the words, 'wherever you enter a house, stay there until you leave the place' (6.10). From now on, as later in the Christian mission, the house is to be the centre of teaching. But there is another difference. We have in fact already seen Jesus teaching in the house at Capernaum, surrounded by crowds spilling out of its walls. But after the parable about defilement in chapter 7 Mark says pointedly, 'and when he entered a house *away from the crowd* his disciples asked him about the parable' (7.17). This is the first time Jesus and his disciples are depicted alone together 'in a house', and on three further occasions (9.28; 9.33; 10.10) Mark emphasizes it as the place of their private instruction, as opposed to the public settings where parables and controversies take place, and to the boat and the road where the disciples' own hardness of heart is portrayed. There is one further time when Jesus and the disciples are alone together indoors: that is the Last Supper. Here the private teaching becomes the ritual that entails inescapable involvement in his death, for now the private instruction of the house and the fearful teaching of the road have come together; from that room the disciples go outdoors and are scattered, eventually re-forming beyond Mark's story to undergo the same hostility from the synagogue that Jesus himself had experienced.

By this stage of the book, however, we are in a denser forest of symbols. From the historical events of the passion, from Old Testament passages seen by the early Church as foreshadowing it, and from his own literary skills, Mark has woven a story 'fraught with background'. Luke and John change his account of the passion considerably, bringing out allusions and meanings not contained in Mark, while Matthew, outwardly staying close to Mark's framework, makes the allusions explicit by his quotations and explanations, so removing much of the earlier Gospel's ambiguity and irony. In the haunting terror of Mark's passion story, however, we are given few answers; we are left instead to ponder, to search and to respond. In Paul the imagery had been dominated by the crucifixion, in which he saw Jesus bearing a curse, dying for the ungodly and reconciling humanity to God, and by baptism, in which the believer is crucified with Christ. The cross stands at the climax of Mark's story too, before which Jesus has called on would-be disciples to take up their cross and follow him. Yet oddly the cross itself does not have the symbolic power that it has in Paul's writings and in later Christian thought and art: the death of Jesus is interpreted mainly through the other symbols that jostle each other in the last six chapters of the book.

First of these is the Temple. Jesus has left synagogues behind, and after chapter 10 he is not shown teaching in houses any more. For now he arrives at Jerusalem, where stands the central building of Judaism. It is the sign of the holy presence of God and of the distinctiveness of the Jewish people. At its heart is the Holy of

55

Holies, which may be entered only once a year by the high priest; at the Temple alone can sacrifice be offered to the hidden God of Israel, and its uniqueness, beauty and splendour are celebrated in psalm and sentiment; its courts are the place of pilgrimage for Jews from all over the world, gentiles being admitted only to the outer one. But in Mark's book this place of holiness has become a place of plotting. In chapters 11 and 12 it is in the Temple that the scribes and priests argue with Jesus (but are worsted in the arguments), that they try to trick him with awkward questions (but fail), that they attempt to arrest him (but have to wait for a darker place and time); it is where Jesus himself peremptorily expels the traders, where he puts unanswerable questions to his enemies and tells his most damning parable. When he comes out of the Temple at the beginning of chapter 13 one of his disciples remarks on its splendid architecture. It sounds like the vacuous remark of a pilgrim from the provinces, but Jesus' reply is devastating: 'Do you see these great buildings? There will not be left here one stone upon another that will not be thrown down.' He is the judge of the Temple. Its religion and its representatives have been found wanting. For all its holiness and splendour the mystery of the Kingdom of God is not in it, and it must be destroyed.

At this point in the Gospel Jesus has just been 'sitting opposite the treasury of the temple' (12.41) judging those who pass by, and is now 'sitting on the Mount of Olives opposite the temple' (13.3) judging the building itself and talking of its impending end. His position speaks for itself: he is seated, he is opposite the Temple staring across at it, and he is once again on a 'mountain'. The fact that this is the Mount of Olives is probably significant too. The prophet Zechariah, who had also written of a king coming to Jerusalem seated on a donkey and of the shepherd being struck and the sheep scattered, prophesied the 'day of the Lord' when in judgement on the nations 'his feet shall stand on the Mount of Olives which lies before Jerusalem on the east; and the Mount of Olives shall be split in two ... and you shall flee ... Then the Lord your God will come, and all the holy ones with him' (Zech. 14.1–5). Later rabbis—and very probably those in the times of Mark and of Jesus—therefore anticipated the Messiah standing on the Mount of Olives and interpreted Zechariah as prophesying that the resurrection of the dead would take place through the split in it. The historian Josephus also records that shortly before the outbreak of war in about 65 AD (and just before the time that Mark is usually reckoned to have been writing his book) a 'false prophet' from Egypt gathered 30,000 people on the Mount of Olives to stage an abortive invasion of Roman-ruled Jerusalem. It is from the same Mount of Olives, Mark tells us, that Jesus enters the city on a donkey, the king coming to judge and being hailed by his people. And it is there too that he will go after the Last Supper. He who judged the Temple will be arrested at his own tribunal and led back to the city to face judgement himself. He prophesied the destruction of the Temple, but it is he who will be destroyed.

In this fearful reversal Mark conceals a riddling meaning, which we shall come to shortly. First let us return to Jesus riding into the city from the messianic throne of the Mount of Olives. Mark writes, 'And he entered Jerusalem into the temple and, when he had looked round at everything, as it was already late, he went out to Bethany with the twelve' (11.11). *Periblepomai* ('look around') is one of Mark's characteristic words, and usually when he writes of Jesus' looking around him it is with the implication that his eyes are piercing in judgement or in anger (e.g. 3.5; 3.34; 5.32; 10.23). So the word carries foreboding; but there is no act of judgement yet, and Jesus leaves the Temple until the next day.

What happens on his second visit, however, is surrounded by the two-part story of the cursing and withering of the fig-tree, which has bothered interpreters from St Matthew onwards. It is part of Mark's narrative method to insert one episode in the middle of another, as when the death of John the Baptist interrupts the mission of the Twelve and the healing of the unclean woman interrupts the healing of Jairus' daughter. Each time Mark means us to interpret the one story through the other; and so it is with the fruitless fig-tree and the desecrated Temple. On the surface it is of course quite unreasonable of Jesus to expect fruit on the tree when 'it was not the season for figs'; but in adding those words Mark is giving a hint that the story must be read symbolically. The tree is left behind abruptly, the curse is as yet meaningless;

Jesus marches on into the Temple and throws out the traders, overturning the tables and chairs. Why? The barren fig-tree tells us: it is because the Temple, sign of Israel before its God, is as fruitless as a tree in the wrong season, or, if you like, it is an old wineskin that will burst if new wine is poured in. The king has come, and the days of the old exclusive Judaism are numbered. To its representatives Jesus quotes Scripture: 'My house shall be called a house of prayer for all the nations.' The Temple is judged, but it is not yet destroyed. On the contrary, the response of the chief priests and scribes to Jesus' act of judgement is to seek a way to destroy *him* (11.18).

But the next morning, as Jesus and his disciples return to Jerusalem, there is a sign: the tree which he had cursed has withered. Matthew, keen on a miraculous effect from Jesus' word, has the fig-tree withering 'at once' on the first day when Jesus curses it, but Mark's interval is deliberate: not only does it allow him to point to the deeper meaning of the curse by moving to the Temple, but it also shows that, as with the fig-tree, there will be an interval between Jesus' judgement on the Temple and its actual destruction (which may have been approaching at the time Mark was writing). So Jesus says to the disciples—and to readers who are wondering how much longer they can endure persecution—'Have faith in God' (11.22). The words about faith and prayer that follow seem impossible to interpret literally, but perhaps they need to be taken even more literally: Jesus points at 'this mountain' (Mount Zion, where stand the Temple and the hostile forces of the old order) and solemnly says, 'Amen, I say to you that whoever says to this mountain, "Be ripped up and hurled into the sea", and does not doubt in his heart but has faith that what he says will happen, it will be done for him.' The interval may seem long, but Jesus has spoken and the mountain that rebels against God's purpose and persecutes the followers of Jesus will at the right time be overthrown and cast down to the depths of chaos. But the time is not yet: Jesus will elaborate on this further in chapter 13, when he will again tell the disciples to 'learn the parable' of the fig-tree (13.28).

After this teaching about prayer Jesus goes on to Jerusalem, and in the Temple the hostilities reopen (11.27). This time the chief priests and scribes and elders take the lead, asking Jesus by what authority he is acting; but he seizes the initiative and will not answer them unless they first answer his question about the authority of John the Baptist. They dare not answer, so neither will Jesus. He has scored a point; but we are left to reflect on what we know happened in the end to John the Baptist. And death looms large in the parable that follows, which again concerns fruit (12.1–11). Unlike the earlier riddles the parable of the vineyard is a clear historical allegory, the vineyard being a common metaphor for Israel: the owner is God, the tenants are the priests and scribes, the servants are the prophets and the murdered son is Jesus. But the owner will destroy the tenants and hand over his vineyard to others: a new Israel is to be formed, for Jesus the rejected stone has become the head of the corner. The authorities get the message and try to seize Jesus. Still his hour has not yet come, and he remains in command in the Temple, confounding Pharisees, Sadducees and scribes—though he commends a scribe who places love above sacrifices. Then he sits opposite the Temple treasury, praising the poor widow's self-giving, before he leaves the building for the third and last time to sit upon the Mount of Olives in judgement and expand upon the Temple's doom.

What can all this mean for us, over 1,900 years after the destruction of the Temple (AD 70) and the separation of the Christian Church from Judaism? Is it worth such a frantic search through Mark's symbolic world? And what business have Christians to be fulminating against Jews—or as in the past doing far more terrible things than fulminating, owing in no small measure to what is written in the Gospels? Do not the implications of Mark's story lead inevitably to Matthew's Jews saying 'His blood be on us and on our children', and so to the horrible and shameful reversal in which the once persecuted Christians became the persecutors?

If we are to persist in unravelling meanings in the last part of this Gospel we must, so to speak, go further into the Temple, right into its sanctuary, in order to come out of it. On one level the Temple in this book is a *building* destined to be destroyed in the Jewish War, and certainly this matters to Mark. But it matters because on another level the Temple is the *sign* of traditional

Judaism, which Mark sees as barren and moribund. And the reason why he sees it in this way is that on another level still the Temple is a multifaceted *symbol*, scattering flashes of meaning through parts of the story where outwardly it does not appear. The clues lie in the three references to the Temple that occur in the passion narrative itself (chapters 14 and 15) after Jesus has judged it. When after Jesus' arrest the Sanhedrin are trying to procure evidence to convict him, Mark tells us that 'some stood up and bore false witness against him, saying, "We heard him say, I will destroy this temple made with hands and in three days I will build another not made with hands"' (14.57f.). The witnesses do not agree and their words are not enough to send Jesus to his death (for that his own words are needed); but when he is crucified the saying is revived in the taunt, 'Aha! you who would destroy the temple and build it in three days, save yourself and come down from the cross!' (15.29f.). Finally at the moment he dies 'the curtain of the temple was torn in two from top to bottom' (15.38). In each case the word *naos* refers to the sanctuary itself, as distinct from the whole complex of temple buildings.

We have already noticed some of the ironies surrounding the destruction of the Temple and the destruction of Jesus. Here they are pelted at us from all sides. The 'false witness' against Jesus is not really false at all; its speakers understand it falsely, but their utterances are inspired truth, like the high priest's question that follows them. What Mark alludes to, John makes obvious, having Jesus say at the beginning of the Gospel after he has cleansed the Temple, 'Destroy this temple, and in three days I will raise it up.' When the literal-minded Jews protest at this, John explains that 'he spoke of the temple of his body', and adds that after his resurrection the disciples remembered and understood this (John 2.19–22). Characteristically Mark is nowhere near so explicit. He lets the symbols work on us in a more haunting way. The Temple whose destruction Jesus decreed was the place where his own destruction was decreed—by the priests and scribes, yes, but by Jesus himself through his words, by the sayings of the prophets and by God who spoke through them. When his body is killed the temple curtain is torn in two and the sanctuary of God's exclusive presence laid open. The *naos*, the focus of God's glory, is now this man's condemned body. And in three days the body will be raised, there will be a new Temple not made with hands which all can enter. But this is no annihilation of the past or of the cross: it remains the body of the wounded surgeon with his bleeding hands and 'sharp compassion'. The body is broken; only so can it heal, only so can it replace the Temple.

Jesus has already referred to his body and its impending death in the house of Bethany (14.8) and in the upper room with his disciples. At this meal he breaks the bread, identifying it with his body, and the disciples eat it. So the temple of his body is broken literally on the cross, ritually in the bread, and symbolically in the disciples. For, having eaten the bread, the uncomprehending disciples are scattered and the Body in which they have been united is immediately dismembered. From now on, in the story and beyond it, the disciples will be, like Paul and his companions, 'always carrying around in the body the death of Jesus' (2 Cor. 4.10), the insiders who are bound up with the destruction of Jesus' body and so must be broken with it. For Mark in his very different manner of writing is as clear as Paul that the Church is the Body of Christ and that the Body must be broken before it can be raised.

Once Jesus' physical body is broken, then, it ceases to be his Body. Joseph of Arimathea went to Pilate and 'asked for the body of Jesus' (15.43). But Pilate gives him not the body but the corpse of Jesus, not *sōma* but *ptōma*, the word used earlier of the corpse of John the Baptist. And when the women come looking for Jesus they are told 'he is not here'. Mark gives no information about and presumably has no interest in what happened to the corpse. But the Body of Jesus has gone ahead where the disciples are told to go, to Galilee, there to be re-formed again and broken again, re-formed and broken again and again in the repeated Eucharist and the mission of the Church. The parable of Body and Temple continues beyond the story Mark tells; but it can continue only in so far as the disciples 'take up their cross' and are prepared to 'lose their lives' in the preaching of good news and the breaking of bread, in the risk of persecution and in generous extravagant service. Two of the disciples there had earlier requested places of honour in Jesus' glory, and he had asked, 'Can you drink the cup

Stumbling on God

that I drink, or be baptized with the baptism I am baptized with?'
(10.38). In ignorance they said 'Yes', and indeed they were right.
But that story of cup and baptism is dark until they do drink the
cup at the Last Supper and Jesus says, 'This is my blood of the
covenant, which is poured out for many.' The cup of salvation is
the cup of death. This is no matter of ritual and symbol only, for
soon after the meal Jesus' life is 'sad to the point of death' and he
prays, 'Take this cup away from me'. It cannot be taken away, for
the words and actions of Jesus in the Temple and the upper room
have not only interpreted but decreed his destiny. And not his
alone. His unwitting companions are bound up with it, eating the
same bread and drinking the same cup. For Mark as for Paul, 'as
often as you eat this bread and drink this cup you proclaim the
death of the Lord until he comes' (1 Cor. 11.26). The body must
be broken and the blood shed, the Church must be crucified.

These symbols of salvation and destruction—Temple and fig-
tree, Body and cup—dart around the final chapters of Mark's
book, interpreting the plain story of a horrible death. Outwardly
it is very plain. Until Jesus leaves the Temple we read frequently
in this Gospel of people being 'amazed' or 'astonished' or 'afraid',
but in the passion narrative these words almost cease; we read
only of Jesus' own great distress in Gethsemane and of Pilate's
'wondering' at the silence and later at the death of Jesus (15.5,
44). The grim story with its mass of symbols and allusions is left
to speak for itself, and *we* (with Pilate) are left to wonder. For
even when this death is interpreted as an act of salvation or a
'ransom for many' (10.45) it is still a thing of horror—all the more
so if we believe that in the Body of Christ we are implicated in it
ourselves—and the interpreting of it in life and in sacrament is
not complete: 'the end is not yet'.

There is one more symbol that stands at the end of the passion
story and also at its beginning, that of anointing. The story of the
anonymous woman anointing Jesus at Bethany is one of those
which Mark inserts between two parts of another story as a sign
that they are to interpret each other. In this case the outer part of
the sandwich is the story of the conspiracy against Jesus. At the
beginning of chapter 14 Mark tells us that it is now two days to
the Passover and that the chief priests and scribes are seeking a

way to seize and kill Jesus by stealth; their efforts are rewarded immediately after the incident at Bethany when an insider, Judas, goes to them, contracts to hand over Jesus and seeks a way to do so. In between these two parts, which set in motion the outward story of the passion, an outsider, an unknown woman, extravagantly anoints Jesus' head. The two stories set side by side point to the contrast between the homage of the outsider and the betrayal of the insider; they also show that we are to interpret the death in terms of anointing and the anointing in terms of death.

Jesus himself says to the people reproaching the woman, 'She has anointed my body beforehand for burial'. But that was not how the woman intended her action. It is the *head* of Jesus that she anoints (a detail altered in Luke's and John's very different versions of this story, where the woman lovingly pours the ointment on his feet). For she is hailing him as Messiah (the Christ, the king, the anointed one), as the crowds did when he rode from the Mount of Olives to the city of David; and the king is consecrated to his office by anointing on the head. No prophet, no priest, no man, but an anonymous woman performs this sacred function, which as Jesus says will be recounted throughout the world. It is similar to the role that Mary will play in Luke's Gospel, bringing forth the Messiah, for which all generations will call her blessed.

Yet unwittingly this woman priest is handing Jesus over to his destruction as surely as Judas is about to, for Messiahship means not political glory but death. When first Peter had hailed Jesus as the Messiah (8.29), Jesus had promptly begun to speak of his suffering and death, and so it is now: in consecrating him as king she is preparing his body for the tomb. The Messiah is 'enthroned through being entombed', as Austin Farrer comments; and there is no way to the Kingdom apart from the breaking of his body. Something is already broken at this anointing, namely the woman's jar (a detail which all the other Gospels omit), and this too may be a symbol of death, alluding to the breaking of the jar at the fountain in the Old Testament preacher's evocation of death (Eccles. 12.6, where the Greek Old Testament uses the same word *suntribō* as Mark does here). Not only dead bodies and kings but holy places too are anointed, as were the Jewish altar, tabernacle and Temple. So when Jesus' body is broken on the cross and the sanctuary curtain is torn in two we know that already the new Temple is prepared and consecrated.

If then we have been reading the story attentively we should not be surprised when another group of women is unable to anoint the body of Jesus on the third day. It has already been anointed for burial: the time of death is now past. The woman at Bethany had come to anoint the Messiah and had found a man who spoke of his death; these women come to anoint a dead body and find a man dressed in white who speaks of Jesus' resurrection. The fig-tree has been cursed, the Temple replaced, the cup has been drained, the Body broken and the King enthroned; but now 'he is not here', and they are too late for the fast God. Jesus does not appear, the women flee in terror and say nothing to anyone, and the Gospel stops in the middle of a sentence. Can this be the mystery of the Kingdom, can this be the good news of the Son of God, that Jesus is absent?

5 *The End is Not Yet*

Mark ends his book suddenly with the words, 'And they said nothing to anyone, for they were afraid' (16.8), which is clearly not a conclusion. We are bound to ask, Where do we go from here? And the temptation is to round things off neatly, as did the later writers who produced longer endings for St Mark (usually printed as appendices to his Gospel in modern Bibles). But that is to treat the book as a biography rather than a Gospel. In the original there is no final triumph, no vision, no joyful reunion. Still Mark makes no concessions to his readers: by ending his book without an ending he is saying to us, What are you going to do about it? He leaves us with the frightened women and the young man's words, to continue the story ourselves but not to end it.

Yet it sounds like good news: 'He has risen'. The king, risen in glory—is this the moment that James and John had been looking for, when they might sit on Jesus' left and right? But 'sitting on the right side', not of a glorious presence but of an empty tomb, is a young man dressed in white. His appearance is that of an angel or messenger of God. But the word *neaniskos* ('young man') takes us back to the only other time Mark used it, when a young man followed Jesus at Gethsemane. That man was naked, casting off his linen garment or *sindōn* as he fled from the presence of the bound Son of God; but here he is seated on the right side of the absence of Jesus unbound, clothed in white as Jesus himself had been in the glory on the mountain. Through these last chapters we are never far from the rustle of clothes being cast off and put on. Jesus' own garments were stripped from him, and the soldiers dressed him, not in celestial white but in mock-imperial purple, before stripping him again, putting his own clothes on him and leading him out to Golgotha. There he was stripped for the third time—his body laid bare, just as he had three times entered and laid bare the fruitless Temple—and his clothes cast away on the gamblers. His body was dressed once more by Joseph of Arimathea in a linen *sindōn*: is this the garment cast away by the fleeing disciple? Whether or not Mark intends us to make the link, the *sindōn*, now a shroud, is also to be cast away in resurrection; it is for a corpse, not a body. At the tomb all is naked and empty. The only presence is that of the young man in white, and he points away from the place of death.

What this man says is obscure, but some at least is plain. Jesus is 'not here'; those who seek him have discovered not a presence but only words. For Mark believes himself to be living in the time of the risen but absent Christ. So he has no image of Jesus 'in the midst' of the disciples as Matthew has, no 'lo, I am with you always', nor has he any image of the Lord's 'abiding' with them as has John. This is made clear in Jesus' teaching on the Mount of Olives. Any who appear now are false Christs, and the disciples must pay no heed to reports of them (13.21f.). The true Christ is not here, and the present is a time for watching and for preaching. Jesus likens it, in his last parable that Mark records, to a period when the master of the house is away on a journey, leaving the servants with their tasks and the doorkeeper in particular with his duty to keep awake (13.33–7). In the next chapter he says to the people reproaching the woman at Bethany, 'You will not always have me'; but at the same time he speaks of the good news being proclaimed in that time of his absence. The Son of Man will come, and indeed the young man at the tomb says that the disciples will see Jesus again; but 'the end is not yet' (13.7), neither the end of time, nor the end of Jesus' story, nor the end of the Gospel.

Most people are probably like the women, fleeing from an absent Christ and preferring a present one, even if dead: a Saviour who is on call. But is this possible without self-delusion? In another story of a journey, *The Pilgrim's Progress*, Hopeful says to Ignorance, 'Why man! Christ is so hid in God from the natural apprehensions of all flesh, that he cannot by any man be savingly known, unless God the Father reveals him to them.' In his austere

Calvinist way, rejecting all idolatry, Bunyan depicts Christian's journey as one *towards* Christ rather than with him. The pilgrimage begins, after Christian's conviction of sin, in an encounter not with Christ but with Evangelist, and even at the cross where he loses his burden Christian does not actually meet his Saviour. Such meetings are mentioned only twice in the course of his journey, and then fleetingly: when Jesus 'came by' and told Moses to desist from beating Faithful, and then, after Hopeful's conviction of sin and repeated praying, in a special revelation to him 'with the eyes of mine understanding'. For the rest, the word of Scripture is enough, and vision lies in the future, in the celestial city. The Calvinist storyteller is as uncompromising as the Carmelite teachers, and as St Mark. Without the absence, the Nothing, there is no beginning.

So we go back to the emptiness of the tomb and the young man's words there. 'Do not be amazed; you are seeking Jesus of Nazareth, who was crucified. He has risen, he is not here; see the place where they laid him. But go away and tell his disciples and Peter, "He is going ahead of you into Galilee; there you will see him, as he told you."' What can be the meaning of this 'Galilee', and how will the disciples see Jesus there? Mark does not tell us, but he allows several meanings to hover around, calling his readers to follow the one who goes ahead out of the story. The word *opsesthe* is the solemn word of vision, as befits an anouncement by an angel, the same word used for seeing the Son of Man coming in glory (13.26; 14.62). So is this vision in Galilee to be the *parousia*, Jesus' glorious return, which he had predicted on the Mount of Olives and before the high priest? If that is so, there is clearly to be an interval, a time of waiting and preaching, of persecution and destruction, before the promise can be fulfilled and the disciples see Jesus. His *parousia* is one meaning of the words that Mark shyly lays on the table, so to speak; and if it is to mean anything to us today we are bound to hesitate as to how literally the words can be taken, recognizing that the interval is far longer than Mark (and Jesus) supposed, and seeing ourselves as still in the time of watching for the signs of future fulfilment. The coming of the Son of Man for Mark is the coming of the Kingdom or rule of God—no longer, as at first in Galilee, in germ and fitful encounter but in its fulness, no longer as 'mystery' but as knowledge; yet still as before not 'in heaven' but on earth. As to how that can be conceived, Mark tells us no more.

The first literary interpreter of the young man's words, however, was Matthew, and he gives them a much more definite meaning. At the end of his Gospel the women obey the command and run to tell the disciples, on the way meeting Jesus who repeats the young man's message. The eleven disciples go to Galilee, 'to the mountain to which Jesus had directed them', and there indeed they see him and are given the commission to make disciples, baptize and teach, and the assurance that Christ is always with them. This seems as far removed from the atmosphere of Mark as it is from the geography of Luke (where the appearances of the risen Christ and the gift of the Holy Spirit take place in Jerusalem). Yet Matthew is following up clues that Mark has laid, in particular when Jesus himself anticipates the young man's words before his arrest, setting them next to the prophecy from Zechariah: 'Jesus said to them, "You will all fall away [or, stumble]; for it is written, 'I will strike the shepherd, and the sheep will be scattered'. But after I am raised up, I will go ahead of you into Galilee"' (14.27f.). The implication is that the shepherd will lead his scattered sheep into Galilee; there the Body broken at the Last Supper and on the cross will be made whole again; and perhaps the promise given by John the Baptist that 'he will baptize you with the Holy Spirit' will at last be fulfilled.

But what Mark says in chapter 13 about the tribulations that lie ahead for the disciples should make us wary of taking the young man's promise in too straightforward a way, predicting as for Matthew a triumphant appearance of the risen Christ which will permanently reunite the scattered disciples and send them out to build the universal Church against which nothing shall prevail. Yes, the men who have drunk from the same cup as Jesus will be baptized with his baptism; but what does this imply? The broken Body will be remade, but only to be broken again in the repeated Eucharist of the disciples and in their mission from Galilee, which, like Jesus' earlier mission there, will be fraught with occasions of stumbling and rejection; and for some of them it will be a draining of the cup to its dregs and the literal breaking of their bodies. There is no room in Mark for an unmitigated triumphalism; nor even in Luke nor in any book of the New Testament, which was after all completed before the conversion of the Emperor Constantine.

But in the young man's words at the tomb there is something else echoing from Jesus' original preaching in Galilee. We saw how outsiders, gentiles even, encountered Jesus with faith and came near to the mystery of the Kingdom of God. Now the despised Galilee carries with it the implications of 'Galilee of the gentiles' (Isa. 9.1), it is the threshold of a world alien to exclusive Judaism; and equally the coming of the 'kingdom of God' carries with it the implication that on that day the gentiles will be admitted to God's presence (e.g. Isa. 49; Mic. 4.1f.; Zech. 8.23; Dan. 7.13f.). For Mark this opening up is anticipated in Jesus' ministry in Galilee of the gentiles, and it is to be fulfilled in the disciples' future mission from the same Galilee after the judgement of the Temple and the death and resurrection of the Body. So the young man's promise is not for the disciples alone, for the insiders who have become outsiders; it is for the gentiles too, the outsiders who are at last becoming insiders.

Already in chapter 5 of the Gospel Mark weaves together anticipations of the resurrection and of the mission to the gentiles. The people of a gentile village, hearing of a disaster to a herd of pigs, come out to the tombs where the tormented madman used to roam and shriek; and they find the man sitting with his exorcist, 'clothed and in his right mind'—as later a young man will be seated clothed at another tomb. This new life in the place of madness and death is too much for the villagers to comprehend; like the women at the other tomb they are afraid, and they ask the disruptive Jesus to go away (5.15–17). But as Jesus gets into the boat to leave gentile territory, the man comes up begging to be 'with Jesus' as one of his disciples. Jesus will not have it. We are used to his telling people to go away and keep quiet after he has healed them; but on this occasion only, in the land of gentile outsiders, he tells the man, 'Go away home to your people and tell them how much the Lord has done for you and had mercy on you.' And, we read, 'he went away and began to proclaim (*kērussein*) in the Decapolis how much Jesus had done for him; and everybody marvelled.' Forbidden to join Jesus and his disciples in their mission to the Jews, he inaugurates the separate mission to the gentiles. And as when it happens in its fulness later, the mission to outsiders begins from the tombs. By contrast, later in the same chapter a Jewish girl is raised from death, the daughter of Jairus the ruler of the synagogue; again people marvel, but here in Israel they are told to keep the good news secret. And so it will be until the third day dawns.

The death and resurrection of Jesus, then, are the moment when what has been kept secret is to be made manifest (4.22); and in a way the events and symbols of death and of resurrection penetrate each other so much that it is not easy to separate them between the Friday and the Sunday. The lamp has been hidden under a tub, it seemed to be extinguished altogether as darkness fell over all the land for three hours. But then in forsakenness and desolation Jesus cries out in the words of Psalm 22 to the God who has not saved him. Fulfilling the words of another psalm, someone gives him vinegar to drink. 'But Jesus uttered a great cry and expired.' The word *exepneusen* means literally that the spirit went out, and perhaps Mark intends us to see in this not only the human death of Jesus but also the release of the Spirit that had descended on him at the Jordan; from Golgotha it goes out into all the world. It is released from his body, and it is released from that counterpart of his body, the Temple, which had claimed to enclose the holy presence of God. For at the moment that Jesus dies the Temple curtain is torn in two, and the gentiles who had been banished to the outer court are admitted to the mystery of the Kingdom of God. The Spirit that has gone out from the body of Jesus immediately fills the gentile soldier who makes the true confession hitherto hidden from all but God and the demons: 'Truly this man was the Son of God'. In all the darkness and agony the light has been put on its stand and the secret made manifest.

But these are symbolic hints: until the third day Mark keeps us in a sombre world of tombs and shrouds and spices. And as we read on to the empty tomb and to Galilee, we may also read back from Jesus' inarticulate cry to his earlier words. In the upper room he had spoken of his blood 'poured out for many'. On the

Mount of Olives, speaking of the persecutions facing his disciples, he had added, 'the gospel must first be preached to all nations'. And in the Temple, throwing the traders out of the Court of the Gentiles, he had quoted the text, 'My house shall be called a house of prayer for all nations.' The events Mark recounts take place for the outsiders, and˙Jesus' life is given as 'a ransom for many' (10.45; like the 'for many' at the Last Supper, this is a Hebraic phrase meaning 'for all'). The purpose of the temple of Jesus' body being broken, of his blood being shed and his Spirit breathed out, is certainly to re-form the Body and gather together the scattered sheep; but that meeting of insiders is only a preliminary to the *outsiders'* being greeted by the good news, being brought into the Body, given the Spirit and the cup of his blood. The holiness of God that had been enclosed behind the temple curtain and the Spirit of God that had descended into the body of Jesus are now released from the breaking-point of Golgotha; yet paradoxically those who are to bear the Body and the Spirit to the outsiders are a foolish group of men who have stumbled and scattered, dependent for the news on a foolish group of women who have fled in terror. What, if anything, happens in Galilee Mark does not tell us, for he wants his readers in their own stumbling way to carry on the story of those women and men.

It is generally agreed that Mark was writing for gentile Christians, and we know from Paul's letters (written well before Mark's book) that the Christian Church was soon planted in non-Jewish communities. The very writing of this Gospel is a sign that the good news has somehow spread from the tomb to the gentiles; yet the broken way the book ends is a sign that its journey from Galilee is still faltering and perilous, like the earlier journey when Jesus went ahead to Jerusalem. For he is far ahead. The spirit follows eagerly, but the flesh is still weak; the Body that is momentarily reunited in an intimacy like that of the upper room is again broken, and many of its members undergo the mockery and destruction that fell on Jesus. If they are to be faithful they will be brought to one boundary after another, cast out of synagogues and meeting in houses, crossing the sea and walking the road and stumbling into the mystery which even when manifest is still mystery, for they cannot hold it:

Here and there does not matter
We must be still and still moving
Into another intensity
For a further union, a deeper communion
Through the dark cold and the empty desolation,
The wave cry, the wind cry, the vast waters
Of the petrel and the porpoise. In my end is my beginning.[1]

Or, as Mark more prosaically puts it, 'the end is not yet'.

Perhaps then the young man's words conceal another meaning still. The Galilee where the reader is to see Jesus is the beginning of the book: from the broken ending we flee in awe and turn back the pages to read again, starting from Galilee where after the baptism and the descent of the dove the story of Jesus begins. And as we read a second time, pausing perhaps more often this time if the rush of 'and' and 'immediately' will let us, we may, so far as 'the natural apprehensions of all flesh' permit, 'see' the hidden Christ, if only his back. For Mark is writing so that we can see. Even on a cursory first reading one cannot miss the command to 'watch' or 'keep awake'. It is solemnly repeated three times at the end of Jesus' words on the Mount of Olives (13.33, 35, 37), where, with uncharacteristic directness, Mark drives the point home by having Jesus conclude, 'What I say to you [the four disciples] I say to all: Watch.' It is repeated twice in Gethsemane to the men whose eyes are 'very heavy'. Not only their eyes but their ears. To them, to the crowd and to the reader, Jesus began his teaching by saying 'Listen!' (4.3), and punctuated it with 'He who has ears to hear, let him hear' (4.9, 23). Yet who has the ears to hear or the eyes to see? Not even the insiders whose hearts are hardened and to whom Jesus says in the boat, 'Having eyes do you not see, and having ears do you not hear?' They do not understand.

But we, Mark's readers, have an advantage over them. Story and symbol are so arranged that if we watch and listen we can be given the mystery that is too hot to hold. Just before the feeding of the four thousand and that conversation in the boat, Jesus had 'made the deaf hear and the dumb speak', taking the deaf and stammering man aside, using his own fingers and spittle, sighing and saying 'Be opened!' And just after the same conversation, when they land at Bethsaida, Jesus leads a blind man out of the village; again he uses hands and spittle, and gradually the man's sight returns. Do you not see? Do you not hear? Eyes and ears can be opened, the tongue released and the understanding given, but only if the disciples follow Jesus 'outside the village', even outside the city to Golgotha. Until that crisis and the good news coming from the tomb the secret is hidden; yet already it peeps out in spasmodic, fleeting encounters, in acts of faith and generosity, in restoration of hearing and sight, in friends removing a roof, in a widow giving a farthing, in a woman pouring out ointment worth thousands of farthings, even in a former lunatic preaching to the gentiles. As we go back to Galilee to see, we are again led out of the story to watch and listen on the shore of our own world.

The solemn word 'listen' occurs again in Mark's Gospel in another episode where hearing and sight are dazzled and the disciples cower in terror (9.2–8). Overcome by the vision of Jesus, Moses and Elijah on the mountain, Peter prattles away about making shelters, for the flesh is weak and needs its sacred canopy, and he wants to domesticate the vision so that it can be managed and enjoyed. But then the cloud overshadows them, and the voice of God declares Jesus for the second time to be his Son, adding solemnly, 'Listen to him'. The words are addressed through Peter and James and John to all the disciples and all the readers: do not listen to the foolish Peter, nor even to Moses and Elijah, but listen to Jesus whose words are in this book. And the point is reinforced when the disciples look round and see 'no longer anyone but Jesus alone with them'. His words do not pass away.

So we are driven back to those riddling words. They are put down in ink by Mark, which makes them seem clear and definite, and therefore we try to construct for them the shelters of official interpretations, saying, 'This is what the parable means.' No matter that those interpretations are often platitudes: we have figured out the mystery and mastered the good news. Why, it is so successful we can even go on to do it with the whole parable of Jesus himself, translating it into neat theories of atonement or programmes of moral enlightenment. It is a heady enterprise, this beating away the strangeness of God. And it is the archetypal idolatry, the failure to watch and to listen.

73

Stumbling on God

We are of course naturally idolatrous, we want a sign. But the seeking of signs is the testing of Jesus (Mark 8.11). His only response is to 'groan in his spirit and say, "Why does this generation seek a sign? Amen, I say to you, no sign shall be given to this generation"'. Our own generation is no different, and failing to receive unambiguous signs we resort to constructing our own and saying they are signs of God: this tremendous experience, that marvellous new book, the latest scheme of ecclesiastical reform. There is the truth, we say. But no signs shall be given, only words and 'mighty works', which are *not* unambiguous but are there for people to stumble on. The refusal of signs and the commands to watch and listen require of us a deep spiritual chastity. Rather than rushing off to build shelters or put the mystery into our own words, we are bidden simply to attend to the words that are laid before us, to pray in desolate places (Mark 1.35; 6.46; 9.29; 14.38), to fast while the bridegroom is taken away from us (2.20) and to perform irrational acts of faith, generosity and service.

To talk and write about God, then, is a foolhardy exercise. Yet it is something that must be done (to paraphrase St Augustine) not so that we may say it all, but lest we keep silent about so overwhelming a mystery. To write about Mark's Gospel is also a foolhardy exercise, particularly when the writer is faced with the temptation, which Mark himself resisted, of providing a conclusion. All we can do is go back to Galilee, retread the road to Jerusalem, see the broken Body and be sent out yet again. We are hurled into the future by the great centrifugal force of Jesus that thunders through Mark's story. What that future contains is not clear. Hints are given. Jesus goes ahead. The mystery is unveiled but not assimilated. All is overshadowed by the ultimate reality of the coming of the Son of Man and by the penultimate reality of the mission to the gentiles.

For us the gentile mission has become history and the second coming myth. Can we still listen directly to this wild story?

Note

1 T. S. Eliot, 'East Coker', *Collected Poems 1902–62*, Faber 1963.

PART TWO

Out of the Story

6 Listening to Parables

After what was said at the end of the first part I had better regard this second one as an appendix rather than a conclusion. But we are left with what might be called the second-order question with which I ended the last chapter, one to which some sort of answer can be provided, before we return to the first-order questions which the Gospel itself puts to us. To those can be given only provisional answers which themselves involve further questions; and the further we go the more the questions and answers will be ones of flesh and blood rather than pen and ink.

Can we still listen directly to this story, coming as it does from a culture so alien to our own? Mark was telling it to a Christian community that expected the speedy return of its Lord and still struggled to discover its identity vis-à-vis Judaism, and he wrote from a background that believed in supernatural spirits and looked for exact fulfilments of prophetic statements made in quite different contexts centuries before. Those are not concerns and thought-patterns shared by many of his readers today. There is in Mark and in the Bible generally this strangeness that necessitates so many layers of translation, interpretation and explanation. We have been giving some quite detailed, even tedious, attention to Greek words and narrative patterns used 1,900 years ago. But is this not futile and sterile? Perhaps if you have read this far you will not entirely think so; but is it not projecting us into the sort of fantasy-world we began by trying to flee? How can we possibly leap over all those layers and respond to the text with the direct attention its first hearers must have brought to it?

Many would say that such an attempt is self-defeating and that we must either treat the Bible as an interesting historical and religious monument or replace it altogether with a scripture of and for our own age. I hope I have been able to show that we need not be driven to such desperate solutions. Certainly, if by 'Scripture' we mean a treasure-chest which is crammed with the answers to all our questions and from which we can extract 'the meaning', then the Bible will eventually bury us in fantasy and anachronism. It is because such methods of reading are held to be correct by so many guardians of the Bible that so many others do not read it at all; and even if they come to church, where you cannot yet escape from its words, they hear them read with glazed looks. But in fact this is a massive *mis*reading of the Bible. It is not that we should instead treat the Bible as literature. The Bible *is* literature. And the stuff of literature is story and symbol, which have not changed substantially in three thousand years. We need eyes and ears, that is really all—though close analysis and historical sense can sharpen our eyes and ears considerably. But neither the listening nor the analysis (in this case, of Mark) will provide us with 'the meaning' of the book, only with meanings. Which is another way of saying that St Mark's Gospel is good literature. What after all is 'the meaning' of *Hamlet* or *The Waste Land* or *The Rainbow*? If anything is worth reading more than once or twice, it can only be because it is built of metaphor and ambiguity. Yes, the exposure of our senses and imaginations to the Gospel's words will certainly jolt us with their strangeness; but that strangeness is not primarily cultural and historical but theological. It was doubtless felt as keenly by those first listeners. For the subject is strange and secret. It is the mystery of the Kingdom of God.

It was in fact too strange already for some early Christians, which is probably why Matthew rewrote and expanded Mark to provide a story more obviously practical for the Church's teaching. Matthew, Luke and John all depart quite clearly, quite deliberately and quite usefully from Mark's original work. They alter the shape of the story and reduce its pace, so that they can include more explicit ethical and doctrinal teaching, and they all end with appearances of the risen Christ. In the case of these three, fairly straightforward answers can be given to the question raised by Mark's title, What is the good news?; though they are still given very much through story and symbol. Jesus is alive and with his followers, God has given us eternal life, Jesus has given himself for us and won forgiveness of sins, Jesus opens up the new Law, and so on. The teaching interprets the story, even disrupts it to proclaim the obvious good news. But with Mark almost all we have is story and symbol. We have to listen and work harder. And such was the success of Matthew and his successors that, despite the great liturgical honour paid to the four Gospels throughout the Church's history, Mark's little book was for long eclipsed by the other three. It may even be that it would not have been kept in the canon of the New Testament had Mark not been thought to be privy to the memoirs of St Peter.

In the nineteenth century critics decided that Mark's was the first of the four Gospels to be written, and it was given much greater attention, in the hope that it would yield really secure historical information about Jesus and his teaching. Those hopes were not fulfilled. But it may be no accident that Mark has received serious attention *as a writer* only in the age of cinema. For he begins and ends his book abruptly; he gives us sudden changes of scene; he has flashbacks, stories inserted within other stories, words and symbols echoing through the book like musical phrases, that fast pace with all its 'and's and 'immediately's. Are not these almost cinematic techniques, and do we not see some of them reappearing in the modern novel, which owes so much to the film? But if we wish to see Mark as a Hitchcock or a Bergman out of his proper age, then we must include also in their fraternity those anonymous authors of Old Testament stories, the economy and allusiveness of whose narrative style Mark inherits as a sensitive reader of the Jewish Bible. What all of them share, whether their images are expressed first on calfskin or on celluloid, is an intuitive grasp of how people listen and respond to stories.

We have a name for Mark, but otherwise he is almost as anonymous as the authors or editors of Genesis and Judges. He probably began his 'literary' career simply as a preacher and story-teller in an early Christian community, perhaps in Rome in the fifties of the Christian era. And we can imagine someone thrilled and challenged by his words saying, 'You must write these stories down'. Anyway, he did so; and in the writing the story-telling was refined and perhaps more carefully structured, without losing the vigour and pace of oral narration. The power of

79

gesture and tone of voice were lost, of course; but in their place he wove a web of symbols that point to meanings in the terse story. How far this was a business of conscious construction and how far a business of the story-teller's intuition we cannot tell; nor does it really matter, for our task is to read and respond to the book, not to investigate its author's psychology. Austin Farrer's Bampton Lectures on inspiration concluded with one on 'the poetry of the New Testament', which was largely a consideration of Mark's writing; it ended by saying, 'The further we go into the question, the more clearly we see that St Mark's words are shaped by a play of images and allusions of the subtle and elusive kind which belongs to imaginative rather than to rational construction.'

Yet while it is helpful to isolate patterns, words and symbols, we cannot—as Farrer himself was tempted to, and as some kinds of modern literary criticism would have us do—treat the book as a self-contained 'work of art', a 'story-world' or 'text' that is its own meaning. Mark refers to actual events of the recent past, however many layers of interpretation may cover them. And above all he refers to the readers' or listeners' present and future. He is not writing to impress or charm but to challenge and convert. It is a Gospel, the Church's book, and so it has been read and reread in solemn liturgical settings for 1,900 years, though admittedly chopped up in the process and overshadowed by Matthew, Luke and John. How many people over the centuries, announcing 'a reading from the Holy Gospel' and reading aloud these stories of Jesus, have not inwardly trembled as their lips proclaimed such terrible words, and perhaps at the end said, 'Can it be so?', as outwardly they concluded, 'This is the Gospel of Christ'?

Can this be good news? Matthew, Luke and John are intractable enough, but Mark's little book is dense and untamed. His Messiah is an anti-Messiah, who dies in agony and is not seen risen. His apostles are anti-apostles, lacking understanding and courage and failing to proclaim good news. Perhaps then this 'Gospel' is an anti-Gospel: the traces of good news in the early part of the book are frequently hushed up by Jesus, those at the end tantalizingly ambiguous. It is not a comfortable book for the religious institution; clearly written in and for the Church, it is nevertheless a Gospel for the gentiles, the outsiders. We have seen

80

how repeatedly the insiders stumble and fall away while the outsiders stumble on Jesus and find salvation; and we have seen how Jesus' death and resurrection, which are the climax of the book, are interpreted as empowering the mission to the gentiles. 'Ah,' says the modern Church, 'mission, outreach: persuading people to think our way and sucking them into our system so we have a nice lot of insiders.' And to that end we have the glossy advertising and the television histrionics. It all seems a long way from Paul in Corinth 'in weakness and in much fear and trembling', or from the little people of Mark's Gospel facing persecution and their crazy acts of generosity.

Yet it is true that the mission is the task of the insiders, that remnant scattered in Gethsemane. In their terror they had stuck the lamp under the tub; now, perhaps trembling as much as ever, they hold it up for the outsiders to see by. But what do we see? A mystery, a parable. In the very act of proclaiming good news, putting it into words, the evangelist shows that he is an outsider to it still. He must be, he cannot possess it, or it would not be *the* good news, news of *God*. As we utter the words they are cast away like a coat on the ground. Some people will stumble over it and kick it out of the way, some will dice over it, some will reverently turn it into a shroud; while others will gaze at it in fascination or terror, and others again will tremblingly pick it up and wear it. The effect of the words cannot be engineered; the moment we speak them we lose control over them. For the parable expresses what cannot be represented. It operates like abstract art, which can arrest and change us, even though it cannot be translated into 'meaning'; or alternatively it can be dismissed as 'just a picture' or 'just a story' and passed by.

But if the story or picture does arrest us then it can impel us, outsiders to its mystery, with our apparently weak and trembling human resources of faith and generosity, impel us in pursuit of the Son of God. Faith is inescapably frail. A true contact with ultimate certainty, we trust, even if only a brushing against its cloak; but a loss of contact with lesser certainties. Stripped and fleeing, the disciple is present at the place where Christ has been. It is paradoxically because of our *horror vacui*, our dread of emptiness and negativity, that so much talk of God *is* empty. We want

81

to cram the foreground with ideas and activity in the hope that we can push away the background, 'the eternal silence of those infinite spaces' that so terrified Pascal in the new cosmology of the seventeenth century (though any who had been aware of the transcendence of God throughout the two and a half millennia previously had also known of that dark background where God lurks). Sadly one can often sense that a preacher, neatly and eloquently sketching the foreground while shunning the back-ground, does not deep down believe in what he is saying. He is trying to order the riddling words and fill the empty tomb, and so they have slipped away from him. And who can blame him? His 'apostolic succession' derives after all from women and men who were just as baffled.

If, however, we seriously reckon with the bafflement, then we are released from an obsessive cultivation of the foreground to watch and listen to the background. It is like treading admiringly round a neat and colourful formal garden, then going through a little gate into an unkempt patch where the walls are invisible and creepers overhang and strange creatures flit about us; and we discover that the wild garden is more real than the elegant one. It has little pattern. We are talking not of 'the faith' or of 'my faith' but of bare faith in the hidden God through the absent Christ. For a world or a Church concerned with its identity and survival the disciple of such a God will often appear a heretic, for he is the one who 'loses his life', while the heretic may often appear a disciple. This is a persistent theme in Mark's Gospel, but one he does not define too closely; for while there is a distinction between 'those of God' and 'those of man' it is not for us to judge and mark boundaries (cf. Mark 9.36–41). Yet in so far as Mark does invite us to judge, it is the *orthopraxis*, the generosity of the widow in the Temple and the woman at Bethany, that counts, rather than the orthodoxy of Simon Peter (and the demons). 'Whoever does the will of God is my brother and sister and mother', says Jesus; and in the course of the book several obscure, irregular and rather unecclesiastical figures are shown 'doing the will of God' and being commended by the Son of God. They disappear as they must, for the disciple of the fast God cannot be static: if one is a 'follower' then by definition one has not reached the goal, one is not yet 'saved'.

Of the nature of the goal we can say little. Mark calls it 'the coming of the Son of Man', which is not our language. Two things however are clear about it. First, it is from outside, the gift of God 'coming with the clouds of heaven', not some construction of our own. The Kingdom of God is something other, something for which the disciples are to wait and watch; yet in another sense its mystery is already given to them (though they can barely receive it) for already the Son of Man has come. Secondly, for all the individual ways and encounters shown in the Gospel, the Kingdom of God in its fulness is public, something to be experienced corporately, in the Body. Mark could have envisaged it in no other way, and later Christian hopes of individual salvation in 'heaven' would have been as incomprehensible to him as to any other New Testament writer: when such hopes did appear in Christian guise they were combated as 'gnosticism'. The resurrection of Jesus is an elusive event, not described or defined in this Gospel any more than in the others; but it is essential to Mark not because it gives assurance of personal immortality but because it empowers the mission to outsiders. Jesus goes ahead and the Body is re-formed to go to the nations, breaking down the divisions of earthly kingdoms in speaking of and waiting for the Kingdom of God.

But that Kingdom is anticipated within the Gospel when the outsiders experience liberating power through Jesus, and in his absence the encounters and anticipations can continue. Such encounters cannot indeed be procured; but sadly they can be prevented, as they are whenever those who honour the name of Jesus banish 'outsiders' or condone the continuing exploitation of the poor. And the possibility of preventing the Kingdom arises too whenever, like Peter, the Church attempts to turn back from the road to Golgotha, trying to defend its Lord from degradation (which is really a refusal of its own degradation); whenever, like James and John, it attempts to turn the glory it glimpses into an opportunity for personal advancement. There is, as we have seen, much subtlety and ambiguity in Mark's presentation of Jesus, but on this point he is utterly direct: 'Whoever would save his life will lose it; and whoever loses his life for my sake and the gospel's will save it.'

As Europe emerges from the Constantinian era, the hearing of the word and the breaking of the bread may be moving again from synagogue to house, as it were; and as this happens it would be odd if some members did not look over their shoulders to the splendour of the past Temple and say, 'What wonderful stones', while others tried to bar the doors of the new house against the lepers and the children. But both of these understandable reactions are attempts to inhabit a fantasy world rather than the shore where the everyday world and the reality of God collide in parable and mystery. The materialism and the nostalgia of our insecure age are affronted by the vision of a man like Mark, who sees infinite value in what is necessarily fleeting and impermanent, and for whom the true disciple is one who watches and listens, gives away her possessions and casts off her cloak. In this Gospel, the Body of the Church is the Body of the crucified Messiah only in so far as it is repeatedly broken and re-formed, broken and re-formed.

There is plenty of evidence that the early Church found it hard to cope with the crucifying evangelical task that Mark evisaged, so we should not be surprised that the modern Church too shies away from it. In different parts of the New Testament, the twentieth-century Christian can quite easily detect features of the Church he knows: the rather clerical and didactic organization that emerges from the Pastoral Epistles, or the tight holy community that lies behind the letters and Gospel of John, or the well-disciplined institution founded on Matthew's rock of Peter, or the enthusiastic, expanding Church of Luke and the Acts of the Apostles. But in the haphazard and ill-defined group of insiders and outsiders who people St Mark's Gospel there is not much that we can recognize as 'Church'. Mark wrote his urgent story for people facing persecution, and it was partly as a response to that experience of persecution that the identity and discipline and hierarchy of the second-century Church emerged—but emerged, it seems, as the opposite of what Mark had tried to advocate. For his broken and re-broken Body embraces suffering and spends itself without regard for its identity; the institution, on the other hand, braces, defines, protects itself against suffering.

But is this not a law of nature? Do we not all want and actually need security, and does not Mark undermine that need, so that the Church was wise to neglect his book in its liturgy and teaching? Non-institutional Christianity is surely as much a chimera as non-institutional politics and as all the utopias of history, so frenziedly sought and so quickly evaporating. Political and ecclesiastical bureaucracies may be stultifying, but at least they are safer and more humane than Robespierre or Pol Pot, the Crusades or the fundamentalists.

Perhaps though we may be looking at the wrong question. What matters may be not so much whether the Church is a movement or an institution as what spirit drives it. Even the many centuries when the Church in Europe was used by the ruling class to sanctify its power and maintain social order did not extinguish the story of Jesus or the symbolism of the Christian sacraments, which ran as a sort of subversive undercurrent below the monarchical or feudal spirit of the institution. Today that spirit is itself moribund. No amount of financial endowment or medieval architecture or sociological musing about 'folk religion' can revive it, and the Church has moved into the religious market-place, jostling for attention among the other creeds, movements and institutions. But the market may prove even more destructive of the spirit of Jesus than the feudal system. For it encourages its stall-holders to polish their images and sell their wares. This means that the Christian gospel is likely to be promoted as a good bargain: security, excitement, even paradise promised as the reward for purchasing 'faith' with the form of words or emotional experience that the particular stall requires. It means that great care and energy are likely to be given to window display, in order to attract new customers and retain old ones. And it means that the customers are likely to need plenty of reassurance that the product (faith) is a valuable possession, and that once they are enrolled they will receive a firm sense of identity and corporate loyalty. So religion as entertainment flourishes at the end of the twentieth century.

Yet it was in the market-places of the eastern Mediterranean that the story of Jesus was first spread. Paul, its most energetic evangelist, saw all those dangers and reacted against them with passion. In his second letter to Corinth he castigated the 'super-apostles' with their eloquent tongues and congenial message and letters of commendation. His own preaching, like his own experience of persecution, promised little emotional reward and little social respectability, but with a perverse chastity he adhered to 'preaching Christ crucified'. Now Paul, a scholar, a mystic and an activist, was no great story-teller; but the story-teller Mark may be displaying the same chastity and fighting the same battles in the cryptic way he writes his book. Can we learn from them both a Christian ascetic for the twenty-first century? And if we are not prepared to, can we expect the glory and terror of the Christian gospel to survive being dissolved in entertainment?

7 *Shedding the Cloak*

To advocate a Christian or any other ascetic today is to go sharply against the spirit of the age. The secular market-place resounds with calls to acquire and to consume, and the religious market-place is not very different, with churches beavering away at their survival or expansion. Is it not arrogant and self-righteous to stand against that spirit, and in any case is it not asceticism also against the spirit of Jesus, who contrasted himself with the sober John the Baptist as 'a glutton and a drunkard'? Traditional Christian ascetical practices—fasting, poverty, celibacy, confession, vigils—have long been suspected by Protestants as a form of 'salvation by works' and sidestepped by ordinary Catholics as an option for the élite. To the rich they seem to threaten the rights of property; to the poor they seem to be acts of religious introversion which do little to forward common justice. Above all, the ascetic is seen as deliberately making himself miserable because of morbid feelings of guilt or impurity.

Now there is indeed much that is neurotic in the ascetical practices of any religion. But their true root lies not in guilt but in desire. To turn to the New Testament again, Paul was a vigorous opponent of any salvation by works but equally vigorous in harshness towards himself. He urges the hedonistic Christians of Corinth to join him in seeing life as a race; and the point of the race and of all the self-control and training that the athletes undergo is to obtain the prize (1 Cor. 9.24–7). This is not merely figurative language: it comes from a man who suffered all the physical hardship that he recounts to the Corinthians. But the 'prize', the 'imperishable wreath' that he seeks in all his fastings and journeyings, in his celibacy, in his insistence on earning his own living rather than claim his evangelist's stipend, is not a personal heavenly reward. 'I do it all', he says, 'for the sake of the gospel', that is, for other people. Paul has not chosen a career as an evangelist, he has been given a commission, and 'Woe to me if I do not preach the gospel!' For that he is prepared to undergo ridicule, poverty and deprivation. The same desire is expressed in a less argumentative way in the letter to Philippi, where he again uses the word *brabeion*, 'the prize of the upward call of God in Christ Jesus'. This prize he has not yet obtained; but its 'surpassing worth' is so clear to him that all his 'confidence in the flesh' and spiritual possessions—his race and circumcision and rabbinic training—are not gain but loss. 'For his sake I have suffered the loss of all things, and count them as refuse . . .' (Phil. 3.4–14). Both in his mystical yearning and in his evangelistic work Paul was drawn in the race onward and upward by this desire for the Christ whose suffering he so manifestly shared but whose resurrection he did not yet share. So urgent and overpowering are this task and this desire that (sounding more like the dedicated terrorists than the sober-suited evangelists of the twentieth century) possessions are simply an encumbrance to him. Ascetical deprivation is therefore not a devotional extra but a logical necessity.

But Paul was by any account an exceptional man. One of the weaknesses that he did not 'boast' of was perhaps his failure to realize that most other people were not exceptional. Could his readers, can we really be expected to enter the same race as he and to run it with the same single-mindedness? Mark, as we have seen, is also uncompromising in his insistence on suffering; at the heart of his Gospel lie Jesus' words to the crowd, 'If anybody wants to follow behind me, let him deny himself and take up his cross and follow me. For whoever wants to save his life [or soul] will lose it; but whoever loses his life for my sake and the gospel's will save it.' But Mark's characters have an ordinariness that might have vexed Paul, and as we accompany them on the journey to Jerusalem that is less an athletic competition than a frightened stumbling along we can perhaps glimpse more vividly the same asceticism and attitude to possessions that sprang from Paul's desiring and living for Christ and the gospel.

Jesus sets out on the journey at Mark 10.17, and it is

accomplished in his arrival at the Mount of Olives (11.1). In between these two points are three encounters and conversations—with the rich man, with James and John and with Bartimaeus—and three passages of instruction to the disciples; at the end is Jesus' entry into the city riding on a colt, and before the journey begins he blesses children, saying that the Kingdom of God belongs to them and to those who receive it like children. Children are unencumbered with possessions and achievements, in strong contrast to the man who runs up and kneels before Jesus just as he sets out on his journey. For all his virtue and ardour, this man cannot receive the Kingdom or inherit eternal life because he 'lacks one thing', or conversely owns many things; unable to give away his material possessions, he is unable to follow Jesus. Despite the perfectly clear words after this when Jesus 'looks around and speaks to his disciples', rich Christians interpret this command to shed possessions as a particular vocation for this one man who is called to the way of poverty and claim that Jesus is not against the possession of wealth but against its abuse. Yet there is no suggestion that the man who went away sorrowful abused his wealth; as a keeper of the commandments he was presumably faithful in almsgiving. Rather, the mere possession of wealth abused *him*, weighing him down like an overcoat from responding to the upward call of God which encounters him in the form of Jesus' journey to Jerusalem. And Jesus applies the man's failure quite generally and quite categorically: 'It is easier for a camel to go through the eye of a needle than for a rich man to enter the Kingdom of God.' The disciples are 'exceedingly astonished' at this, but they need not feel personally threatened by the saying, for, as Peter says to Jesus, 'we have left everything and followed you'. For this renunciation, says Jesus, there will be rewards, both 'now at this time' and 'in the age to come'; but they are double-edged ones, for with the 'houses and brothers and sisters and mothers and children and lands' (not individual possessions but the shared life of the Church) are promised also persecutions, and through the whole exchange of renunciation and reward runs the principle of reversal—'many that are first will be last and last first'.

With this barbed encouragement the journey continues, Jesus

walking ahead, the amazed disciples behind. For the third time Jesus speaks to the Twelve about what is to happen to him in Jerusalem. The Son of Man will not cling to dignity or even to life; and two at least of the disciples cannot absorb this, asking for positions of state in his Kingdom. But this whole world of status and power must be renounced along with material wealth. As after the conversation with the rich man, so after the reply to James and John, Jesus speaks in general terms of the cost of discipleship and then of his own destiny: 'For the Son of Man also came not to be served but to serve, and to give his life a ransom for many.' The lure of a place of honour can be as strong as that of money or land, perhaps all the stronger to those who have 'left everything' and are willing to accept the cup and the baptism: the apostle with his privileged access to the leader and the priest in his intimacy with holy things are continually being distracted by their spiritual possessions and enticed to flaunt them so that they can be served rather than serve, basking in the beauty of holiness that veils the exercise of power. All this too must be renounced: 'it shall not be so among you'.

The journey continues through Jericho, where an outsider interrupts it. Mark implicitly contrasts the blind beggar Bartimaeus with both the rich man and James and John before him. He has only one thing, his cloak, and he wants only one thing, his sight. The cloak that the rich man and James and John could not shed he throws on the ground, and the one thing he lacks he receives, not as a possession but as sight with which to 'follow him on the road'. As the journey continues after this third encounter there is no general instruction of the disciples; the episode is followed instead by the acted parable of the Messiah entering the city on a colt, echoing Zechariah's prophecy (which Matthew quotes) of 'your king coming to you ... humble and riding on an ass'. The last act of the Gospel now begins, its protagonist shorn of all possessions material and spiritual; he will as he predicted be mocked, spat upon and scourged, and in the end see his last hope expire as he cries, 'My God, my God, why have you forsaken me?' The road that Bartimaeus takes up is the *askēsis* of the Son of Man. Mark lays it before his readers and obliquely asks them to risk it too.

So the Gospel is a warning as well as an invitation. If you stumble on God and are swept up by desire for his rule, then you must be prepared to shed your cloak, perhaps whole layers of clothing, prepared to be naked as Jesus at Golgotha or the young man in the garden. And the cloaks are not only those of wealth and status, that the rich man and the sons of Zebedee cling to. There are others, of knowledge and experience and religion. As soon as these good things are turned into possessions—'*my* religious experience' or '*the Church*'s faith'—they impede our road ahead and distract us into the complicated business of defending our property. We have seen from Mark's stories how this happens with material wealth and spiritual status, and the same thing can happen to religious people and institutions with their doctrinal and intellectual possessions. How easily the sparkling images of the Bible and dogmas of the Creed are grasped and turned into stale systems that supply their owners with the arrogance of certitude. But like the millionaire's, their reward is a sour one, for the possessors of true doctrine have to busy themselves with burglar alarms against infiltrating heresies and insurance policies against inconvenient new knowledge. And all the time the system is being protected and elaborated, it engages less and less with the blind beggars for whose benefit it ostensibly exists and less and less with the glory and terror of the God who is its ostensible subject. The fruits of bigotry and exclusivity that stem from this possessive approach to doctrine are well known, and it is all the sadder that they frequently arise from a genuine zeal attached to genuine symbols of transcendence. But the most vibrant symbol will be forbidden to express itself once it is turned into an embroidered decoration and sewn into the right place on the doctrinal coat to bolster the owner's intellectual security. Christian doctrine is at its heart a kaleidoscope of *moving* symbols, metaphors and parables, and the business of descriptions and propositions needs to be firmly subsidiary to it. If the Spirit of God is free, then any verbal formulation must be tentative and provisional. The intricate coat must be cast off and the symbols set free if our minds are to move forward on the road of Christ's *askēsis*.

An even more popular kind of possession is that of experience.

The religious person likes to find some reward for his adherence to the way, and emotional uplift is often simpler to procure than intellectual certainty. Having experienced it (whether through music, through friendship, through speaking in tongues—all of them good things) I am tempted to cling to this warm cloak as evidence of my acceptance by God or progress towards him. But that too I must cast off if I am to be free to move forward in desire for God and his justice. The uncompromising Spanish mystic St John of the Cross, teaching this radical detachment, speaks of 'the night of the spirit' as well as 'the night of the senses'. It is not that 'religious experiences' are bad; but they are not God, and as soon as the religious person turns them into a possession to cultivate and protect they drag her down. For St John's 'ascent of Mount Carmel' as for St Mark's journey to Jerusalem it is essential to travel light: 'a soul must strip itself of all creatures and of its actions and abilities (of its understanding, taste and feeling) so that when everything unlike and unconformed to God is cast out, it may receive the likeness of God.' And the 'night of the spirit' is not only active but passive; that is, according to John, as well as the soul's refusal to cling to spiritual consolation there is God's refusal to grant it, in his persistent wooing of the soul from the created to the Creator.

But this talk of 'the soul' can be very dangerous. Even the soul that is detached from external possessions and experiences can become concerned for itself, its own purity or relationship with God; and sadly much that goes under the name of 'spirituality' does not share the insistence of John of the Cross (and of Mark) on the soul's being stripped even of its own selfhood. A concern with my own soul's health and my personal fulfilment, however devout or austere may be the programme, is perhaps the most insidious form of attachment, for it diverts me into myself, away from both the glory and terror of God and from a neighbourly and political concern for others. St John of the Cross applies his offensively clear verses to all stages of the journey:

> To reach satisfaction in all
>   desire its possession in nothing.
> To come to possess all

desire the possession of nothing.
To arrive at being all
    desire to be nothing.
To come to the knowledge of all
    desire the knowledge of nothing.
To come to the pleasure you have not
    you must go by a way which you enjoy not.
To come to the knowledge you have not
    you must go by a way in which you know not.
To come to the possession you have not
    you must go by a way in which you possess not.
To come to be what you are not
    you must go by a way in which you are not.
When you turn toward something
    you cease to cast yourself upon the all.
For to go from all to the all
    you must deny yourself of all in all.
And when you come to the possession of the all
    you must possess it without wanting anything.
In this nakedness the spirit finds its rest,
for when it covets nothing,
nothing raises it up and nothing weighs it down,
because it is the centre of its humility.[1]

This reiteration of nakedness and nothing is an anti-mysticism rather like St Mark's anti-Gospel; and both arise in part from the experience or threat of persecution, which strips us of our soul whether we will or not. 'For whoever wants to save his soul will lose it, but whoever loses his soul for my sake and the gospel's will save it.' The ultimate possession that I must renounce is my own salvation.

Perhaps the earliest and most powerful aberration from the way of Jesus was the construction of Christianity as a religion of individual salvation. Whether it comes in a fully-blown supernatural version, with individual sentences by the Judge to hell or purgatory and individual seats in heaven, or in a secularized version based on moral righteousness or psychological fulfilment, it involves the refusal to 'lose one's soul' and to serve rather than

93

be served. To undertake the holiest or most altruistic activity for the sake of my own salvation or satisfaction weighs down and perverts the activity. Conversely, there are few forms of self-worship more virulent than the one to which many Christians are prone, of contemplating their personal worthlessness or sinfulness. The encounter with Jesus as Mark presents it expels that concern with self and sin: the haemorrhage of twelve years ceases, the wild Gerasene no longer lacerates himself. And Jesus himself is not an unassailable soul living in perfect communion with God but a body broken and destroyed, crying out, 'My God, my God, why have you forsaken me?'. That body is raised, not to be a companion to the individual disciple but to go ahead to the gentiles, opening up to them the baffling disruptive world of parable and cross.

And if he goes ahead, Jesus too cannot be the possession of the soul or of the Church. Judas alone kisses him; his enemies alone hold him; and the tomb is empty. The desire to possess the Christ as an indwelling presence 'abiding in you', which derives from the fourth Gospel, is fraught with danger, both for the individual believer and for the Church. For if I believe that Christ dwells in me, through faith or through sacrament, then I easily grow liable to complacency; the one who should be leading me on to new risks of faith and generosity becomes constrained by my own desires and fears, and I can imagine or even boast that I am 'saved'. Similarly, if the Church or a part of it identifies itself with the Christ or sees him as the invisible crown of its hierarchy, then it remains liable to the religious imperialism that has marred so much of its history, loath to admit the possibility of its being in error and prepared to chastise heretics and unbelievers in the name of its Christ. This is not what Paul meant when he talked of 'the body of Christ' and 'living in Christ'. That Body, as in Mark's Gospel, is one which is scattered and destroyed; being baptized 'into Christ Jesus' means being 'baptized into his death', and living 'in him' means being 'made like him in his death'. Christ is indeed for the Church that is his Body—in order not to console it but to strip it, so that it too can be free to give itself 'a ransom for many'. The only identification possible is the one that renounces possession.

Private possession, then—whether of material wealth or of religious status, of correct doctrine or experience, of my own soul and its salvation or of Jesus himself—is an attempt to destroy the freedom of the thing or person possessed. It is a denial of the mystery of what is other than ourselves. The paintings immured in Japanese bank vaults are outwardly unchanged, but they are prevented from expressing themselves, their value has become a monetary one only. So it is with the most precious 'spiritual' goods, so with Jesus, if we try to enclose them and annihilate the distance between ourselves and the other. Without space there can be no movement, without distance no sense of the holy or operation of the parable. A painting of the Annunciation by Lorenzo Lotto shows a modest bedroom, with the homely paraphernalia of candle and bedclothes. Into this scene has flown the unearthly archangel, conventionally winged and holding a lily, but alive with windswept hair and sky-blue eyes and garments, genuflecting before the Virgin while holding one arm aloft to where, above and outside the room, God the Father reaches from the clouds. Mary herself, in front of her bed and prayer-desk faces the viewer in an enigmatic gesture which can be interpreted as one of either self-protective fear or positive acceptance, perhaps of both: hands half parted, her body kneels, but her head and eyes are not downcast. And in the very centre of the picture, glancing in terror at the invading angel, a cat scuttles to hide beneath the bed. Here biological reality and divine glory meet. But it is an encounter without embrace, in which hands are not joined and persons remain distinct, in terror or respect at each other's presence. In this vision, incarnation involves neither the domestication of God nor the etherealization of woman. Nor is it an encounter to savour as 'religious experience': the whole posture of the figures shows a tremulous readiness to move forward.

How little chastity we have, how eager we are to tame the terror and destroy the distance, so that the encounter can be shut up in an album and need not project us onward. Mark's story ends and ours begins with the women at the tomb, unable to see or hold their beloved. Conservative Christians rightly stress the importance of the empty tomb, but for the wrong reasons. For it proves nothing about the nature of resurrection, whether it be 'physical' or 'spiritual'; it provides no assurance, nothing that can be possessed or understood. 'He is not here.' In the young man's words and the tomb's emptiness is the ascetic rejection of the world that wants to clutch goods and possess knowledge—and the ascetic space to be filled with the immensity of God and his Kingdom. That is the starting-point for the journey to Galilee. If we take it up, calling ourselves 'Church', what possible tasks can be ours, what identity can we claim as followers of this elusive God?

Note

1 From 'The Ascent of Mount Carmel', *The Collected Works of St John of the Cross*, trs. Kieran Kavanaugh and Otilio Rodriguez, Washington D.C.: ICS Publications, 1973.

8 Going into Galilee

To say, 'Christ is risen', means inevitably to say also, 'He is not here'. Not in the tomb, nor in Jerusalem, nor in the Church, nor in bread and wine, nor anywhere. He has become, in Paul's words, 'a life-giving spirit', no longer bound and held by place, not imprisoned Prospero but free Ariel, moving, going ahead. So the risen Christ can be nobody's possession, not Joseph of Arimathea's, nor Pilate's, nor Peter's, nor the Church's. The veil has been ripped in two from top to bottom, and the secret is exposed to the gentiles; there are no more insiders.

Yet while it is necessary, if we must have definitions, to talk of the resurrection as 'spiritual', it is necessary to talk of it as 'physical' too—or, better, 'somatic'. Paul writes of the *sōma pneumatikon*, the spiritual body; and a body has shape and form, however dispersed it may be and however unclear its boundaries. Christ the life-giving spirit is identified with but not contained or exhausted by his Body. For Paul, the Body is to begin with the diverse collection of Jews and gentiles, rich and poor, wise and foolish, zealous and self-indulgent people who make up the churches he knows so well; but potentially it is the entire creation (Rom. 8.21–3). For Mark, it is to begin with the men who eat Jesus' body and drink his blood and then fall away and are scattered and called ahead to Galilee; but jostling around this Body are the outsiders, women and men, tax-collectors and sinners, who sit at table with him or stumble on him, and around it too are the myriad gentiles, foreshadowed in the demoniac, the Syrophenician woman and the centurion, for whom also the good news is proclaimed. The boundaries and standards of membership are uncertain, but the Body is real: Christ is not discarnate, and the mystery of the Kingdom is revealed not primarily in solitary contemplation but in human encounter.

This can be verified not just from study of the New Testament but from everyday experience, particularly the experience of those who have the task of evangelism. The 'evangelist' who imagines that he possesses a clearly defined product and that those who buy it are saved need not detain us; fortunately there are others who know that in proclaiming 'good news' they are handling mystery and who respect the otherness of those they address. And these pastors and preachers are continually being humbled and taken aback by the simple people who are wiser than they and the poor people who are richer than they. Parables sparkle and convert, though they are unauthorized; healings take place, though the name of Jesus is not mentioned; the oppressed are liberated and walk free, though the liberators may be called atheists and the oppressors Christians. Again and again the outsiders barge into the story of salvation. Again and again the Christian evangelists or insiders find their expectations reversed and recognize the life-giving spirit in unlikely situations. The story of Jesus has caught hold of them, they cannot abandon it; but it is continually being expanded for them, the shape of the broken Body continually being changed. The evangelist's task is not to turn 'the world' into 'the Church', not even to make disciples as an end in itself, but to recognize, name and celebrate the fast Son of God as he runs through the world.

To insist on the 'Christian' label, then—as when some fervent believers feel that every course of action must be justified from Scripture or that they should go only to a Christian doctor or a Christian grocer—is an attempt to hold down the Son of God within clearly marked territory, and that means quenching the free Spirit. The Body wants to maintain its integrity; but it cannot do so, for its destiny is to be broken. It is natural enough for the Church to want to polish its image and stick its label on its works like any other organization. But this sits oddly with its claim to be the Body of the one who came as a deacon, not to be served but to serve; for the good deacon or servant does not frantically draw attention to himself but watches and listens, working unobtrusively like the salt in the stew or the hidden seed that leads to the full grain.

This is still in terms of general principle, however. *In what ways* is the Body to serve? When in Mark's Gospel Jesus sends out the Twelve it is in order to preach, to exorcize and to heal. Lest this be seen in terms of triumphant achievement, Mark inserts between the sending of the Twelve and their return the account of the fate of that earlier evangelist John the Baptist; after the return (the only occasion when Mark calls them 'apostles') is the feeding of five thousand men in which they assist. And though modern Europe is far removed from the villages of first-century Galilee, the picture of the apostles in Mark 6 provides a powerful agenda for the Church's evangelistic service in the twenty-first or any other century: preaching and calling to repentance, casting out spirits, healing and feeding, the whole being overshadowed by the risk of persecution. It will not be and never has been easy to 'endure to the end' in such service, patiently standing with the sick or hungry or possessed in the name of the crucified Son of God, watching and working for their release. And because of the greater complexity of modern society and the fact that so many of the spirits requiring exorcism take up their dwelling in institutions as well as persons, the agenda is bound now to be political as well as domestic. This need not require the Church to maintain large agencies and programmes for development, education and medicine, let alone to form Christian political parties; in most countries there is no reason why the service of Christians should not be given through that of secular bodies, including those of the state. But it does mean that those who claim to live by the way of Jesus must be prepared to preach, exorcize, heal and feed in the public arena. The preaching and call to repentance may be in the ascetic protest against a society that trusts in possessions and weapons and in the refusal to worship its false gods. The exorcizing may be in the public exposure of and determined opposition to the people and forces which abuse power and dehumanize their fellows. The healing may be in the practical advocacy of the rights of those who are handicapped or inadequate or poor; the feeding in lobbying and symbolic action to contest the maldistribution of natural resources between and within nations. The details of the evangelistic agenda are not to be written down in books but worked out in the situations which confront each person and community that claims to follow the way of Jesus; if it takes a form at all like what I have outlined it would be odd if the evangelists did not undergo the threat of sporadic persecution.

This may all sound very earthly and 'unspiritual', though it is after all on earth and not in heaven that Mark's readers are to watch and listen for the coming of the Son of Man, and not many of the encounters in his Gospel are overtly religious in content. So does the task of the Christian evangelist differ at all from that of any other person of good will? Is there any visible shape to the Body, or is it completely diffused in the world?

Where Jesus *is* named is in the three activities that are distinctively Christian (thought not so arcane that 'outsiders' are excluded from them), namely the telling of the story, the sharing of the meal and the baptism in water. Simply by giving importance, first, to the story of Jesus, a listener responds in some degree to the attraction of its central character, identifying herself with the way that Jesus lives and dies, even though she might still hesitate to call herself Christian. And those who not only give importance to the story but hear and re-hear it as 'the gospel' in the Church's liturgy do so because they have identified themselves to a fuller degree, if perhaps still very fearfully, with the one whose Body is broken in it. We have seen how that story can come to life when attended to with faith and imagination—all the more so when it is not just listened to but interpreted through preaching, art, drama or study. We have also seen how its episodes can collide with our own stories and experiences, so that the distance between England and Galilee is compressed: we become characters in the story of the Son of God; he becomes the leader in our own struggles and encounters. So the story spills out of the pages of the Gospels, heard and broadcast in innumerable other lives which acknowledge Jesus.

This whole task of apprehending and evangelizing is expressed, secondly, in the sharing of the meal by which Christians re-enact the story of Jesus. Why it should be a meal is not as obvious as at first it seems to those brought up in the Church. In Mark's account of the Last Supper there is in fact no command of Jesus to 'do this in remembrance of me'. Instead (as in Matthew's account but unlike Paul's) the giving of the cup is followed immediately by the words, 'Amen, I say to you, no more shall I drink of the fruit of the vine until that day when I drink it new in the kingdom of God'—that is, when all secrets are finally made manifest and all human rule destroyed. This suggests that if the meal *is* to be repeated (and presumably Mark knew that it was and participated in it) it is repeated as a celebration of and cry for the coming of God's rule: it is an anticipation rather than a memorial. Yet in anticipating the Kingdom the eaters also identify themselves with the Jesus who was killed in the past. What Paul expresses in his pregnant saying that in eating the bread and drinking the cup 'you proclaim the death of the Lord until he come', Mark expresses in his story of the disciples, gathered for the meal, eating the body and drinking the blood, then stumbling and scattering and leaving Jesus alone. The pattern is to continue after Jesus has gone ahead into Galilee: the Body is to assemble, to name Jesus, rehearse his story, eat and drink and then disperse, bearing the Body of Jesus in the world that kills it, watching and working in his name for the coming of the eucharistic Kingdom.

This poses many questions to the Church that shares the meal today. Despite the great benefits of liturgical reform, the celebration of the Eucharist is in most churches still very cultic and verbose. The sense of remembrance is real and often poignant. The sense of anticipation, however, is muted in the worshippers' attempt to adore and hold fast the present Christ. Feeling that we should be affirming our 'personal relationship with Christ', we shy away from being led by him from the table into Gethsemane and Galilee. Yet scattering and mission are what the Mass is for. The words Jesus speaks at the Last Supper identify its actual food and drink with his body and blood. The eaters are aligned therefore with the one who is to be mocked and spat upon and scourged and killed: they are to risk losing their life for his sake and the gospel's, through preaching, exorcizing, healing and feeding that may invite literal persecution. And lest this sound like the call to heroic and romantic martyrdom, there are troubling echoes from the psalms that suggest the eaters are identified also with God's enemies, 'who eat up my people as they eat bread', the evil-doers who 'came upon me to eat up my flesh' but 'stumbled and fell' (Pss. 14.4; 27.2). One of the company at the supper actually plots

101

with Jesus' enemies; all the rest fail and flee. We are what we eat; we also destroy what we eat. And those who share in the meal today are both disciples and traitors, for however strong their commitment to the eucharistic way of Jesus they are implicated also in the world whose moral and economic values oppose that way: the most ardent member of the Body of Christ cannot fail to belong also to the body of humanity. In celebrating the Eucharist no one can avoid this continued tension between destroying and being destroyed, forming the Body and breaking the Body, and so 'proclaiming the death of the Lord until he come'.

But the Last Supper is not the only meal recorded by Mark and the other Gospels. The words about Jesus' blood shed 'for many' are interpreted in earlier meals, where, to the horror of scribes and Pharisees, Jesus eats and drinks with tax-collectors and sinners, and in particular in the two meals in the desert where the crowds are miraculously fed. The eucharistic giving and sharing, then and now, is not for the sake of a community qualified by the correct morality, education or ritual: it is an open table. As with the manna in the earlier desert, all receive the same share, for in this anticipation of the Kingdom wealth and poverty are abolished and still bread is left over. But unlike the manna of the Old Testament, this broken bread is for all—the gentiles as well as the unclean and sinners of Israel. Jesus does not exclude. But the scandalous openness of his table means that the materially or religiously wealthy will exclude *themselves* if they cannot repent, going off like the Pharisees to murmur, plot and destroy. It is probably no accident but a tribute to the power of the meal even in its sanitized cultic form, that it is often the wealthier Christian congregations which seek a 'simple' non-eucharistic form of cele- bration, the utter simplicity of the meal of Jesus being rightly perceived as a threat to their private property. For the poor and rejected, however, the Eucharist should be the celebration that demons are being cast out, that the Kingdom is coming which was foreshadowed in the Exodus and Law of Israel and in the radical egalitarianism of Jesus: a celebration that is nevertheless fleeting, for Jesus cannot be held and the Kingdom has not yet arrived. The food at the table is holy, and the presence is real; but precisely because it is holy it cannot be contained, either in the tabernacle or in the heart of the believer. The Body is broken and scattered to do its subversive work in the world that kills Jesus, struggling against 'the leaven of the Pharisees and the leaven of Herod' about which he warned in the boat.

For rich and poor alike, the cost of this celebration and scattering is high; and it is perhaps therefore a proper instinct that has led the Church from early times to erect barriers and standards for admission to communion. But the irony is great when this is set against the indiscriminate hospitality of Jesus. Nowhere is it more apparent than in the reluctance of most churches to admit young children to share in the Body of him who said that the Kingdom of God belonged to such as them. True, the young child can scarcely grasp the cost of belonging to the Body. But then what adult can? Even the twelve companions of Jesus, according to Mark, had drained the cup before he told them what it contained. Young children, barred from the table, have however been welcomed at the font by the 'mainstream' Christian churches, and the baptismal sign of the cross, the mark of persecution, has even become a mark of respectability. Though the historical reasons for this traditional way of administering the two 'gospel sacraments' are understandable, it is a strange reversal of the practice of Jesus, who apparently welcomed all to his table but called few to actual discipleship. For the symbolic drowning of the candidate in baptism expresses public commitment to the *askēsis* of Jesus, to losing life for his sake and the gospel's, which is only hinted at in the Eucharist. It could be that the Church's practice will change, as some radical Protestant groups and some more traditional Asian churches are already suggesting, so that outsiders will be indiscriminately invited to the open table, where Jesus is named and the Kingdom is anticipated, that for some this will lead into the ascetic risk of eucharistic living and sharing of goods, and from there may lead further into the commitment of baptism, deliberately becoming 'insiders' with the evangelical tasks of preaching, exorcizing, healing and feeding.

However the Church's sacramental practice develops, it is unlikely that the story of Jesus will cease to attract and disturb and turn things inside out, and unlikely that women and men will cease to find themselves involved in the story and led out from it into Galilee. And so the story will grow. But attention to the roots is still needed if the growth is not to be perverted and the name of Jesus reduced to a cypher or slogan. That is why I have been implicitly maintaining that whether or not Mark's Gospel has chronological priority among the four it must have theological priority. The 'hard reading' comes first. If the glory and terror of the unseen God have any reality, then we must resist the calls for precise definition and clear instruction—resist them because they reduce symbol, metaphor and parable to intellectual systems and the way of the cross to a book of rules; resist them because they are an idolatrous attempt to vanquish the strangeness of the Kingdom of God; resist them in the name of Jesus and even if they bear the *imprimatur* of St Matthew. Refusing to accommodate ourselves to the world's clothing, dare we travel light from the tomb into Galilee and beyond, bearing our troubling message? And if we dare, will the promise finally be fulfilled, that 'there you will see him'?

Epilogue The Sparkling Shore

This book is one of 'theology'. It belongs, in other words, to the subsidiary activity which interprets the ordering of living symbols that we find in preaching and poetry and creeds. And the preaching, poetry and creeds are themselves subsidiary to the living of the story in flesh and blood and the venturing out of the story into the immensity of God and the cry of his world.

Now, however much it is inspired, the Bible is only a part of the symbolic power through which we encounter God, and St Mark's Gospel is only a part of the Bible. But exposure to the impact of Jesus in Mark is as necessary as exposure to the theology of the cross in Paul if Christians are to avoid the delusions of triumphalism, whether it be the conviction that I am an insider, already 'saved', or the belief in the infallibility of my church or system of doctrine. It is the negative way that comes first. 'Nothing, nothing, nothing, nothing, nothing, nothing, and even on the Mount nothing', as St John of the Cross inscribed on his sketch of the 'mount of perfection'. Without that chastening of mind and spirit we shall be substituting an idol for God and substituting our own gratification for service to the world.

Perhaps out of deference to their forefather Aristotle, or perhaps because it makes it less obvious how far they are generalizing, literary critics have a habit of reverting to Greek when they want to make definitions. Joining their sodality for a moment, we could think of Mark as being *parabolē*, Matthew as *didachē*, Luke as *muthos* and John as a distillation of all three: parable, instruction and history/myth. *Didachē* and *muthos* provide valuable, memorable and often beautiful patterns by which we can better

105

apprehend the invisible subject who is greater than either; but they are built on *parabolē*, on the collision of disparate realms that is the mystery of the Kingdom of God. And—to continue the Greek vocabulary—the *parabolē* uses to the full the techniques of polysemy (writing that expresses a multiplicity of meaning) and parataxis (the Hebrew narrative style of linking actions together with little comment or causation), both of which give a sense of disjunction but also a freedom and a challenge to the reader's imagination. The parables of Jesus and Mark's whole parable of Jesus, with their feet planted both on the mountain and in the humdrum world, inevitably stretch us. But if we bear the tension and continue to watch and listen, the parable can bring us nearer both to the glory and terror of the hidden God and to the concrete world in its activity and its pain. There will be repeated dislocation, but there need be no contradiction, between persistent reaching out to God and generous immersion in the political and domestic world. It is much more comfortable, of course, to lie in a hammock between the two. The negative way *is* negative, it begins at the tomb in flight from emptiness; but it is nevertheless from there that we are led to Galilee, the positive proclamation of good news and the fruitful service of a world in need of food and healing and the casting out of spirits.

And exposure to the parable can alert our eyes and ears to the parables that still lie in wait all around for us to stumble on and falteringly interpret. In the collision between my frail glasses and the untamed forces of nature, the question thundered at me again through the radiant obscurity: 'Do you still not understand?' And of course we still do not understand. Faith does not provide but seeks understanding, and faith is the attentive, generous response to the parables that litter our shores. And if it is also Christian faith, those parables are interpreted in relation to the great and terrifying parable of Jesus.

A man in Jericho who was far blinder than I and who had to beg for his living was sitting by the road. A famous healer was passing by, and the beggar shouted out, 'Have mercy on me!' People told him to shut up, but he persisted, 'Son of David, have mercy on me!' And the Son of David who was Son of God stopped and told the people to call the beggar. He cast off his cloak—which he depended on not just for warmth but to collect his alms—jumped up and ran to Jesus. In reply to his urgent and beggarly request Jesus said, 'Your faith has saved you', and told him to go away. 'And immediately he received his sight'; but instead of going away he 'followed him on the road'.

The road led straight to the Mount of Olives, to the Temple, to Gethsemane and Golgotha and Galilee, one reversal after another. Mark does not tell us any more about Bartimaeus. He is just an outsider who comes to life for a brief moment. Fleetingly, gloriously, he is there with us in that broken Body which is the Communion of saints and sinners.

A Note on Books

The Gospel sends its readers out into action, not into academia. But books can help us in the search for right knowledge and right action. Here are some that are related to the themes of this book.

A very readable *introduction* to Mark is in Luke Johnson's compendium *The Writings of the New Testament* (SCM/Fortress 1986), pp. 147–69, which also contains a full bibliography. A longer and very stimulating one (unfortunately translated too late for me to take account of) is Bas van Iersel, *Reading Mark* (T. & T. Clark 1989).

Among more conventional *commentaries* on Mark, the most useful for the ordinary reader are probably those by H. Anderson (Marshall, Morgan & Scott 1981) and D. Nineham (Pelican/SCM 1963). Those with Greek can also consult the commentary by V. Taylor (2nd edn, Macmillan 1966).

Innumerable *articles* have been written on Mark. Some important ones are collected by William Telford in *The Interpretation of Mark* (SPCK/Fortress 1985); and another interesting selection is in *Interpretation* XXXII.4 (Oct. 1978). Two articles worth hunting out are by C. F. Evans, 'I will go before you into Galilee' (*JTS* V [1954], pp. 3–18); and by John Fenton, 'The Passion Narrative in St Mark's Gospel' (in James Butterworth ed., *The Reality of God*, Severn House Publishers 1986, pp. 21–32).

Other *books* about Mark, written from a variety of viewpoints, include:

R. H. Lightfoot, *The Gospel Message of St Mark*. Clarendon Press 1950.

Austin Farrer, *A Study in St Mark*. Dacre 1951.

T. J. Weeden, *Mark—Traditions in Conflict*. Fortress 1971.

David Rhoads and Donald Michie, *Mark as Story: An Introduction to the Narrative of a Gospel*. Fortress 1982. This also contains a fresh modern translation.

Ernest Best, *Mark: The Gospel as Story*. T. & T. Clark 1983.

John Drury, *The Parables in the Gospels*. SPCK 1985.

J. L. Houlden, *Backward into Light: The Passion and Resurrection of Jesus according to Matthew and Mark*. SCM 1987.

On interpretation of the Bible generally and the minefield of 'hermeneu-

A Note on Books

tics', some useful books (listed roughly in order of increasing complexity) are:

David Jasper, *The New Testament and the Literary Imagination*. Macmillan 1987. This contains a helpful bibliography.

Sallie TeSelle, *Speaking in Parables: A Study in Metaphor and Theology*. SCM/Fortress 1975.

Austin Farrer, *The Glass of Vision*, the Bampton Lectures on inspiration, prophecy and poetry. Dacre 1948.

Robert Alter, *The Art of Biblical Narrative*. Allen & Unwin 1981. On the Old Testament.

Frank Kermode, *The Genesis of Secrecy*. Harvard UP 1979. Contains among much else a stimulating reading of Mark.

Northrop Frye, *The Great Code: The Bible and Literature*. Ark Paperbacks 1982.

Stephen Prickett, *Words and 'The Word': Language, poetics and biblical interpretation*. CUP 1986.

The discussion of the sacraments in Chapter 8 above draws partly on ideas from Timothy Gorringe, *Redeeming Time* (DLT 1986), especially chapters 8 and 10.